KEY
WOMEN
WRITERS
EDITOR SUE ROE

CHARLOTTE
BRONTË

CHARLOTTE BRONTË

PENNY BOUMELHA

Jury Professor of English
University of Adelaide

INDIANA UNIVERSITY PRESS
Bloomington and Indianapolis

Manufactured in Great Britain

Library of Congress Cataloging-in-Publication data are available from
the publisher

ISBN 0-253-30107-6 cloth
ISBN 0-253-25455-8 paper

1 2 3 4 5 94 93 92 91 90

For Patricia Ingham

Key Women Writers

Series Editor: Sue Roe

The *Key Women Writers* series has developed in a spirit of
challenge, exploration and interrogation. Looking
again at the work of women writers with established
places in the mainstream of the literary tradition, the
series asks, in what way can such writers be regarded
as feminist? Does their status as canonical writers
ignore the notion that there are ways of writing and
thinking which are specific to women? Or is it the case
that such writers have integrated within their writing
a feminist perspective which so subtly maintains its
place that these are writers who have, hitherto, been
largely misread?

In answering these questions, each volume in the
series is attentive to aspects of composition such as style
and voice, as well as to the ideas and issues to emerge out
of women's writing practice. For while recent developments in literary and feminist theory have played a
significant part in the creation of the series, feminist
theory represents no specific methodology, but rather

Charlotte Brontë

an opportunity to broaden our range of responses to the issues of history, psychology and gender which have always engaged women writers. A new and creative dynamics between a woman critic and her female subject has been made possible by recent developments in feminist theory, and the series seeks to reflect the important critical insights which have emerged out of this new, essentially feminist, style of engagement.

It is not always the case that literary theory can be directly transposed from its sources in other disciplines to the practice of reading writing by women. The series investigates the possibility that a distinction may need to be made between feminist politics and the literary criticism of women's writing which has not, up to now, been sufficiently emphasised. Feminist reading, as well as feminist writing, still needs to be constantly interpreted and reinterpreted. The complexity and range of choice implicit in this procedure are represented throughout the series. As works of criticism, all the volumes in the series represent wide-ranging and creative styles of discourse, seeking at all times to express the particular resonances and perspectives of individual women writers.

Sue Roe

Contents

Acknowledgements   xiii

Introduction: Plotting the ground   1

1 *The Professor*   38

2 *Jane Eyre*   58

3 *Shirley*   78

4 *Villette*   100

Notes   123
Bibliography of works cited   141
Index   149

Acknowledgements

The University of Western Australia granted me a six-month study leave in 1988 which enabled me to write this book and for which I am grateful. I should like to thank audiences at the University of Western Australia, the University of Adelaide and the Frank Kermode Seminar at the Humanities Research Centre, Canberra, for their stimulating responses to versions of some of these chapters. I am grateful to *Southern Review* and to its editor Deirdre Coleman for permission to reprint Chapter 2.

More personally, a number of friends and colleagues read chapters for me and offered encouragement and ideas, for which I must thank them: Hilary Fraser, Patricia Ingham, Andrew Lynch, and especially Ian Saunders, whose rigorous scrutiny and critical acumen were generously given, even when he would no doubt rather have been working on Hawthorne. Catherine La Farge saved me a long wait by sparing some time for research on my behalf in the Bodleian Library, and Tim

Dolin drew my attention to a number of useful references. Janet King was unfailingly cheerful and efficient at the word processor, Bruce McClintock helped with proof-reading and indexing, and Sue Lewis was as helpful and kind as she always is. I am grateful to Sue Roe and Jackie Jones for inordinate patience. And a special thank you to Catherine Boumelha.

Introduction: Plotting the ground

'La vie d'une femme' (Villette, p. 182)

Charlotte Brontë has maintained a place amongst the more widely read and studied authors ever since the initial publication of *Jane Eyre*,[1] even if F.R. Leavis's assertion that 'there is only one Brontë'[2] – and that one Emily – suggests that it is by mere accident of siblinghood. And in particular, she has never ceased to be read by women: feminists of the 1920s and 1930s regarded *Shirley* as an inspiration, schoolgirls of the 1950s and 1960s studied *Jane Eyre* as a set book; feminist critics of the 1970s and 1980s have used *Villette* as an exemplary text for pedagogic purposes. From first publication to the more recent developments of feminist criticism, it is true to say that Brontë, more than most, has been perceived as a key *woman* writer. Her audience has on occasion been presumed female: *Shirley*, one contemporary reviewer remarked, is a 'book which women will admire as very passionate and which

1

men may regard as somewhat prosy'[3] (even though, according to another, 'her women . . . can never be accepted as real ladies'[4]). More interestingly, as Ruth Gounelas has shown, 'nine of the fifteen prominent reviewers of *Jane Eyre* in 1847–9 spent time examining the "feminine" or "masculine" aspects of the novel.'[5] Then as now, there was no common agreement as to what those qualities might actually be, but certain ideological trends reveal themselves fairly readily. *Jane Eyre* is found to exhibit both 'charm' and 'power', whether it is thought to be the work of a woman or of a man.[6] One reviewer, convinced that the book is written by a woman, nonetheless counts among its strengths 'masculine power, breadth and shrewdness' and among its faults 'masculine hardness, coarseness, and freedom of expression.'[7] Later, reviewers of *Shirley* found it variously to be 'womanly' and 'pleasing' and to have 'charm'; to show 'intellectual analysis' as Currer Bell's main strength, even though 'plainly she is deficient in humour'; and to combine the 'hand of a woman . . . endowed with the finest and, we trust, the most tender sensibilities of her sex' with 'the intellectual power of a man'.[8]

In such cases, the presumptions and attributions of masculinity and femininity are attached (along predictable lines) to specific qualities of the novels rather than to the sex of the author. Nevertheless, I think it is undeniable that they are generated and permitted by that disturbingly ungendered pseudonym 'Currer Bell'. What is of primary interest here is the perceived importance of the question of the author's sex in itself. Whatever the answers arrived at – a woman, a man, the product of joint authorship – the question is rarely allowed to pass unasked by contemporary reviewers.

Some of those who joined in the initial speculation about the sex of Currer Bell relied upon the central subject matter of *Jane Eyre*:

> Who, indeed, but a woman could have ventured, with the smallest prospect of success, to fill three octavo volumes with the history of a woman's heart?[9]

Others looked to the characterisation of Rochester, that 'portrait of a man drawn by a woman' and of St John Rivers, 'another example of the woman's pencil.'[10] Some took their starting point in the author's unmistakable acquaintance with the minutiae of women's lives (an argument not altogether dead, as Pauline Nestor's remarks on *The Professor* attest[11]); others again in the equally unmistakable absence of such an acquaintance:

> No woman . . . makes mistakes in her own métier – no woman trusses game and garnishes dessert-dishes with the same hands, or talks of so doing in the same breath. Above all, no woman attires another in such fancy dresses as Jane's ladies assume . . . No lady, we understand, when suddenly roused in the night, would think of hurrying on 'a frock'. They have garments more convenient for such occasions, and more becoming too. This evidence seems incontrovertible.[12]

All these varying incontrovertible answers serve only to reinforce the importance of the question. But while no conclusions about the *kind* of man who might have written *Jane Eyre* seem to strike these reviewers as necessary, the woman who could have done so is impugned either as 'one who has, for some sufficient reason, long forfeited the society of her own sex'[13] or as 'a woman pretty nearly unsexed'.[14] That is to say, while the reputation of the novel need not suffer from the promiscuous commingling of 'masculine' and 'feminine' elements outlined by its reviewers, the reputation of its female author was certain to do so.

In this context, it is useful to look at the discussion of *Shirley* by G.H. Lewes, who was a little later to see George Eliot through similar vicissitudes and speculations. Lewes was among those reviewers of *Jane Eyre* who was confident that he had detected the work of a woman, despite the 'power', 'mastery' and 'knowledge of life' that it seemed to reveal and which might more conventionally have been attributed to a male author.[15] Later, however, despite his personal acquaintance with Brontë, he amended his assessment, deploring in both *Jane Eyre* and *Shirley* the flaws resulting from an 'over-masculine vigour'.[16] He is prepared, in his opening remarks, to defend women against the widespread imputation of intellect inferior to that of men, on the grounds that 'the position of women in society has never yet been – perhaps never can be – such as to give fair play to their capabilities' (p. 160). This, however, is not due to inequalities produced by social organisation and reinforced by social expectations; it is, rather, the result of a biological destiny, since 'the grand function of woman, it must always be recollected, is, and ever must be, Maternity' (p. 161). Although not all women fulfil this particular function – 'virgins and childless widows' might be allowed to follow intellectual or artistic pursuits, the reader might think (p. 161) – 'it is impossible to know who are to escape that destiny, till it is too late to begin the training necessary for artists, scholars, or politicians' (p. 161). Nevertheless, he concedes that women have distinguished themselves in literature. The problem with even the best among them – 'second only to the first-rate men of their day'

(p. 162) – is an interesting one; it is that they have 'often written from the man's point of view, instead of from the woman's' (p. 162):

> Women have too often thought but of rivalling men. It is their boast to be mistaken for men, – instead of speaking sincerely and energetically as women. So true is this, that in the department where they have least followed men, and spoken more as women, – we mean in Fiction, – their success has been greatest. (p. 162)

Feminists will probably not be surprised, incidentally, to hear that Lewes finds it 'worthy of a passing remark, that women have achieved success in every department of fiction but that of humour' (p. 162).

In these remarks preceding his actual review of *Shirley*, Lewes brings conveniently together a number of assumptions and lines of argument. Writing should be directly connected with the ideologies of gender and the sex of the author, or else what is praiseworthily 'masculine' becomes culpably 'over-masculine'. Women have unused capabilities, and deserve a 'fair play' which it is nonetheless impossible to accord them, since what disqualifies them from the exercise of those abilities lies not in society but in nature. Women writers should write 'sincerely' – that is, apparently, in a way held to be representative of their sex – for to do otherwise, to adopt a masculine tone or a man's point of view, is a limiting and potentially confusing form of impersonation (even though male writers had virtually from the beginning of the novel taken for themselves the freedom to write as female narrators or from female points of view). In any case, writing is, for a woman, a denial of purpose and design, a denial of the 'grand function' of the reproductive organs to which even 'virgins and childless widows' should sacrifice their capabilities.

Small wonder, then, that Brontë's response to Lewes's comments on her work was 'God deliver me from my friends!'[17]

Nor was Lewes's a unique perspective. Some of what he has to say resurfaces later, sometimes in surprising places. Leslie Stephen, for example, despite his appreciation of some aspects of Brontë's writing, nevertheless found her both narrow and (as Lewes suggested) humourless.[18] His daughter Virginia Woolf in turn echoed these criticisms in her own accounts of Brontë, as among those 'self-centred and self-limited writers' who do not 'attempt to solve the problems of human life' and are 'even unaware that such problems exist.'[19] Later, Woolf attaches her sense of Brontë's narrowness unequivocally to the sex of the writer, and in doing so attacks her from the opposite direction from that chosen by Lewes:

> In *Middlemarch* and in *Jane Eyre* we are conscious not merely of the writer's character, as we are conscious of the character of Charles Dickens, but we are conscious of a woman's presence – of someone resenting the treatment of her sex and pleading for its rights. . . . It introduces a distortion and is frequently the cause of weakness.[20]

The explicit feminism here deplored in *Jane Eyre* had already been detected in earlier responses to each of the novels. The heroines of *Shirley*, for instance, 'both suffer from the malady of unrest and dissatisfaction, – on the prevalence of which among women of the nineteenth century so many protests have been issued, so many theories of "emancipation" have been set forth.'[21] And, famously, Matthew Arnold could find in *Villette* 'nothing but hunger, rebellion and rage' beneath an inadequate cover of 'fine writing'.[22]

In all these ways, then, Brontë's writing has from the

first been tied to her sex, and therefore in turn to a whole range of assumptions and arguments about questions of gender: a key woman writer indeed. Most particularly, analysis of and speculation on the *kind* of woman she was has always figured largely. Gounelas points out how in both Stephen and Woolf, Brontë's status as a 'parson's daughter' is invoked for its relevance, if not even its explanatory power.[23] Some kind of response to and assessment of her as historical individual is commonly central to the discussion and evaluation of her writing. Parson's daughter, romantic schoolgirl fantasist, isolated and self-generated artist, frustrated spinster, sister to Emily, keeper of Branwell: all of these have become almost too familiar to us. And to them, more recently, more feminist-influenced work has added the motherless and oppressed daughter, the woman seeking work and independence, the seller-out to a loveless marriage, the martyr to pregnancy. So it is, then, that Brontë has been made into an exemplum of the lives of women or a paradigmatic woman writer. The effect of this has often been to stand the novels in the shadow of what is, plainly, a life that has been fascinatingly construed. I have little to say here about the writer herself. 'Charlotte Brontë', in this book, designates for the most part an *oeuvre* rather than an author. This is not because the historical individual is of no interest to me – indeed, I have read the biographies as avidly as anyone else[24] – but because there is nothing new I could add to the stories of her life, and because I have tried, in general, not to repeat what has been widely discussed elsewhere. Nor, I should say, do I deal with her juvenilia, primarily because the adult novels are more widely available and certainly much more widely read.[25]

My own project in this book is, I suppose, a double one: to offer readings of the novels, and also to engage with some of the major issues within feminist criticism as it has been practised. The kind of attention Brontë has received has often been based on the way in which her work can be made so readily to display those elements central and valuable to the various versions of the so-called 'Anglo-American' feminist critical tradition:[26] strong heroines, women earning their own living, feminist polemic, outcrops of the Gothic, rage, subversive wit, challenges and modifications to romance. Much good and detailed criticism has been produced in these areas, and I have not wished to repeat it, though I have tried wherever possible to direct the reader towards it. One result of this kind of focus, however, has often been that the identification of heroic individuals as bearers of feminist anger or argument has resulted in undue concentration on that sincere and energetic writing-as-a-woman sought by Lewes and the occlusion of other significant social and textual issues such as class and race. I have tried in my own readings (and particularly in the cases of *Shirley* and *Jane Eyre*) to shift the ground towards these areas. In general, I have chosen often to attend to plot as an important element of the historically specific possibilities of writing within the novel form.

'Tolerat[ing] the drivelling theorists' (The Professor, *p. 215*)

Arriving at a grand public concert in Villette, Lucy Snowe catches sight of a group of figures coming toward her: 'a handsome middle-aged lady', 'a gentleman who might be her son', and with them, in pink and black, 'the third person' (*Villette*, p. 189). The group is soon recognised as another of Lucy's repeated self-confrontations, as an image in the mirror, and 'the third person' – characteristically the person of realist narration – is Lucy herself. What she reflects, and reflects upon, in this incident is not merely herself, but 'myself as others see me' (p. 189). Now Lucy is also, as we know, ' "nobody's daughter" ' (p. 130), and I shall go on to discuss below the suggestion that this confers upon her a status outside patriarchal determinations. But there is also, here, another point to be made. Elizabeth Ermarth has argued that the realist narrator 'is "nobody" in two ways . . . .: it is not individual, and it is not corporeal.'[27] In such a context, to take as a narrator 'nobody's daughter', and to make of 'the third person' a moment of self-division and self-reflection, is to pose the problem of the positionality of that unindividuated, disembodied voice. In other words, it is to undo the ease of consensus that such narrators serve to potentiate. And it is, further, to raise the question of the relation between 'woman as a narrated group'[28] and the woman who writes her own life: she who speaks and she who is spoken are placed in uneasy confrontation.

In each of Brontë's novels, there is at least one figure of the woman as artist, artist as woman: Frances Henri writes empathetic narratives of exile and lost birthright, Jane Eyre paints mysterious images and writes her autobiography, Shirley Keeldar composes allegorical accounts of female power and, with Caroline Helstone, is an unwritten poet, Lucy Snowe buries the letters of uncensored self-expression and provides instead an oddly self-conscious, edited autobiography.

And in each novel, too, there is a certain emphasis upon bilingualism and translation, questions of mother-tongues and linguistic mastery. It is by learning the language of the male lover (whether it be English, French or Hindustani) that Brontë's orphaned, exiled heroines can establish their place in the world. But at the same time, their bilingualism is less a sign of linguistic dispossession than the index of a particular proficiency empowering the double speech of their stories. Patricia Yaeger has commented upon the 'utopian moment' of the 'space within language which had not been there before' as among the interruptive, emancipatory strategies of which Brontë avails herself; like good feminist critics, the Brontë heroines span the hermeneutics of suspicion and the poetics of celeb-ration in their relation to the cultural 'languages designed to consume them'.[29] There is a striking con-nection, in these protagonists, between writing and being under male surveillance. So, Frances Henri and Shirley Keeldar both learn to compose in the language of their lovers in the form of the *devoir* – a school exercise, certainly, but also to be translated as a duty, an obligation. Jane Eyre, watching the Rivers sisters translate Schiller, nevertheless herself comes under the eye of their brother St John. And Lucy Snowe is made to write under the gaze of the school inspectors, just as she is obliged to conceal her uncensored letters from their prospective male reader. That the male gaze is the site of relations of power is now virtually a commonplace of feminist film criticism. The point is succinctly put by E. Ann Kaplan:

> To begin with, men do not simply look; their gaze carries with it the power of action and of possession which is

lacking in the female gaze. Women receive and return a gaze, but cannot act upon it.[30]

Clearly, to transfer this theory from the literal seeing of the cinema spectator to the metaphoric context of the literary text is potentially a risky manoeuvre, although Kaplan in any case includes in her preliminary definition of the gaze the look of men at women within the film text itself. Nevertheless, watching is no less an act of interpretation than reading, and the continuities and reciprocities of cultural texts are such that I do not find it an illicit transfer. The look of sexual difference, then, is the look of power, and the scrutiny under which Brontë's women write is an inscription of the conditions of possibility of their texts. Those who become, within the context of their own fictive status, narrating women, the autobiographers of Brontë's fiction, do so when they have placed themselves, or have been placed, beyond the purview of the male gaze: in her schoolroom for Lucy Snowe, and isolated at Ferndean with a man who sees only dimly at best and a son who seems to have 'inherited his own eyes' (*Jane Eyre*, p. 457) in the case of Jane Eyre. The third-person, narrated heroines, Frances Henri and the two female protagonists of *Shirley*, have relinquished the creation of stories by the end of the novels in which they appear.[31]

We might see in all of this the registering of that 'double intertextuality' which Nancy K. Miller has suggested is the specific characteristic of women's writing: that is to say, its interconnectedness to traditions of women's writing and of writing by men, its emergence 'from the "wild zone" of female experience' and its unavoidable passage through 'the *symbolic* economy of the dominant culture embodied in the structure of its language'.[32] For Miller, 'gender signatures' may be inscribed in a text in a number of ways: in a self-consciousness about the singularity of the heroine and the identity of woman, for example; in a dissenting relation to the plots and, more specifically, modes of closure available to the heroine, constrained though the text in question may be by the demands of genre; or, again, in the staging of scenes of desire and/or scenes of writing figured in a woman-controlled, anti- or non-patriarchal space.[33] I am not convinced that, as signatures of the sex of the author, these cannot be so to speak 'forged'; what they denote, rather, might be a certain recognition of the ideological conditions of possibility of feminist writing. And in this, such 'signatures' suggest a very useful way in to the particular interest of Brontë's manipulation of plot.

Plotting was more than once singled out by Brontë's contemporaries as a failing in her writing. The largely sympathetic reviewer Eugène Forçade commented of *Jane Eyre* that 'the plot, here is the weak side of the work. . . . I cannot understand why she should have thought she needed to have such complicated and disjointed incidents, often improbably linked.'[34] And Lewes, in his review of *Shirley*, made a similar complaint, of a lack of that firmly established sequentiality one might expect of a novel:

> The book may be laid down at any chapter, and almost any chapter might be omitted. The various scenes are gathered up into three volumes, – they have not grown into a work.[35]

To this he added a further objection: that the proper sequence of plot is disrupted by episodes such as what he calls 'a really remarkable tirade about Milton's Eve . . . an eloquent rhapsody' (p. 168). The 'rhapsody' is among those elements in the novel which, for him, 'betray a female . . . hand' (p. 169). And we find the same word recurring among the reviews of *Villette*:

> Allowing for some superfluity of rhetoric . . . . – and for one or two rhapsodies, which might have been 'toned down' with advantage – this tale is much better written than *Shirley*.[36]

'Disjointed incidents', in Forçade's words, and 'eloquent rhapsody' in those of Lewes: it is the relation between the two, between sequential plotting and rhapsodic dilation, that interests me about Brontë's plotting and I have chosen to concentrate on it to some degree in the chapters on *Shirley* and *Villette*.

The great explanatory theories of the nineteenth century, after all, are narratives: whether we speak of Darwin, of Marx or of Freud, we speak of theories which, by means of emplotment, make chronological sequentiality reveal itself as – or become – immanent structure. As Peter Brooks has pointed out, the secular plotting of the nineteenth century, with its search for significance through authoritative beginnings and causal evolutions, foregrounds 'historical narrative as par excellence the necessary mode of explanation and understanding'.[37] Hence the vital interdependencies in this period of those discourses and modes of writing predicated upon the explanatory power of serial structure: archaeology, autobiography and biography, evolutionary biology, the realist novel and, of course, history. What these might be said to share is, in Tim Dolin's words, 'the desire for a continuous re-affirmation of the commonality of experience',[38] a sense that the individual life is comprehensible and meaningful on the basis of a shared narrative structure. And further, the very mode of narration characteristic of the realist novel (what Ermarth calls the 'heroic recollection of an invisible and dematerialized narrator'[39]) has been seen as one of the primary and most powerful ideological constituents of the form in the nineteenth century:

> The genial consensus of realistic narration implies a unity in human experience which assures us that we all inhabit the same world and that the same meanings are available to everyone. Disagreement is only an accident of position. However refracted it may be by point of view and by circumstance, the uniformity at the base of human experience and the solidarity of human nature receive confirmation from realistic conventions. All individual views derive from the same world and so, with enough time, problems *can* be solved, tragedies *can* be averted, failures in communication *can* be overcome.[40]

In this sense, emplotment might be seen as an activity that both calls upon and calls up a consensual agreement of reader and text. But if the very readability of plot is its enactment and guarantee of such hermeneutic affinity, then the nature of the society in which those readers are grounded and those stories are made means that the affinity begins and confirms itself within the terms of gender. That is to say, in those great explanatory emplotments that are, say, the descent of man or the Oedipus complex, the readability of the narrative rests upon the commonality of an experience presumed, explicitly and implicitly, to be male, or at least to belong to men.

Since the sequential explanatory modes of history and biography are so intimately embroiled with ideological postulates of the nineteenth century, it is perhaps scarcely surprising that the historical novel and the biographical form of the *Bildungsroman* should be among its major forms of fictional narrative. Fredric

14

Jameson, arguing that behind the textualised histories to which alone we have discursive access there nevertheless lies something more, has urged that 'History is what hurts, it is what refuses desire and sets inexorable limits to individual as well as collective praxis';[41] and Leslie Rabine has defined a 'feminine historicity' as the desire on the part of the female subject 'to enter the historic process and to become an active agent of history'.[42] In the negotiation of these two points, the necessary desire and its inexorable limitation – perhaps equivalent to what Brooks names a 'male plot' of ambition and a 'female plot' of resistance and waiting[43] – it is possible to locate in the process of emplotment the focus of a certain ambivalence common in women's writing in this period: a sense that in order to produce the comprehensibility of structure, it is necessary to resort to the readability of plot, and hence to accede to evolutions and causalities that are oppressive, constricting.

Jane Austen, for example, already illustrates this with a fine irony: some key words of *Pride and Prejudice*, 'want' and 'design', create a sardonic blur at the point where desire and plotting interact, and the Bennet couple act out an inseparable mismatch in which Mrs Bennet forever speaks the fatuous foreseeability of plot – it is very likely that Bingley *may* fall in love with one of the daughters, it *may* rain and force Jane to spend the night beneath his roof – whose necessity Mr Bennet at once recognises and scorns. George Eliot, too, betrays a scepticism about the construction of plot, mounting, for example, a 'Final Rescue' of her aspiring heroine in *The Mill on the Floss* by means of a flagrantly engineered flood that cannot be faulted on the grounds of rhetorical prolepsis but also marks an exasperated *impasse* of typical sequentiality.

We see here, then, the dilemma of plotting for these women realist writers: its painstaking construction, in the appeal to typicality and plausibility, of a hermeneutic consensus with a community of readers is simultaneously undermined by its flaunting of a shapeliness that betrays the constraints of simplification and repression. What cannot be plotted, the realist novel seems to suggest, must be 'abandoned to illegibility'.[44] Now, the conventions of narrative do not politely halt at the boundaries of writing; clearly, they encode and transmit interpretations and expectations of other kinds. Between the use, transformation and refusal of well established literary tropes and devices, and what can be said, asked and imagined within social relations more largely conceived, there exist complex interdeterminations. The telling of stories raises issues crucial for feminism as for other kinds of oppositional politics: issues of representativeness and representability, of selection and occlusion, of speaking and being spoken for. The sense of a story untold has lain behind much of feminist criticism and historiography, and that 'other side of a well-known tale' has often been taken as the equivalent of 'the elements of women's existence that have never been revealed', as DuPlessis puts it.[45]

In such a view, it seems that narration might in a relatively unproblematic way reveal and restore what has been concealed and suppressed in patriarchal societies. But it is precisely here that Brontë's experiments with form and genre are of interest. According to Peter Brooks, 'if "secret lives" are to be narratable, they must in some sense be plotted',[46] and the question of available plots brings with it some revelation of determinacy. Brontë's heroines, great readers as they

are, sometimes seem to have embarked on a project of
rescuing what escapes plotting: Jane Eyre reads the
pictures rather than the text in the books that she loves
as a child; and Lucy Snowe reads books whose pages,
censored by the excisions of M. Paul, have been
rendered no longer sequential. But Brontë's attempts
to make narratable the 'secret life' of women, both her
plots and what in her novels might be said to *resist*
plotting, compel us to recognise that the legibility of
her heroines for realism depends upon their imbrication in plotting. What makes them readable for us
leads them also to the ' "ordinary destiny" ' (*Shirley*,
p. 174) of typicality, and so, in a society in which the
heterosexual couple has been the site of meaning of
woman, toward the plot of romance. But to concede
this is not necessarily to hand Brontë over wholesale to
sentimentalism or fatalism or patriarchal ideologies.
Even the same old stories can after all be ironically
inflected, knowingly quoted, in such a way as to throw
their axiomatic status into question. Miller makes a
similar point:

> By female plot I mean quite simply that organization of
> narrative event which delimits a heroine's psychological,
> moral and social development within a sexual fate. . . .
> Female plot thus is both what the culture has always
> already inscribed for a woman and its reinscription in the
> linear time of fiction. . . . It comes to us, of course, from
> male as well as from female imaginations – *Pamela*, say, or
> *Madame Bovary*. But female-authored literature generally
> questions the costs and overdetermination of this
> particular narrative economy with an insistence such that
> the fictions engendered provide an internal, dissenting
> commentary on female plot itself.[47]

By common agreement of much feminist criticism, it

seems, it is in the Gothic strain within the realist text that the repression by sequential structure of the unplottable and disorderly force of feminine desire finds expression. Or at least, such has become a common enough reading of, say, Jane Eyre's madwoman in the attic or Lucy Snowe's nun. I want to suggest in the chapters that follow, though, that it is not only to such excrescences of plot that feminists might look for the histories of the unnarratable; that what Jameson calls the 'reaudition of . . . oppositional voices'[48] can also come about by our attending to the suspicious and sceptical mode of their plotting itself. This, then, is my own design in looking here at those elements of Brontë's fiction that might seem to conform fairly and squarely to the sequential explanatory drive of so much of nineteenth-century writing and at the ways in which they are formed and troubled by the focus on women. In this way, I hope to bring together some consideration of the historically specific meaning of writing as a woman, and something of our present sense of the nature and urgency of questions of gender. In the chapters that follow, I shall consider Brontë's use of the form of the historical industrial novel in *Shirley*, and of the *Bildungsroman* elsewhere. First, though, I want to turn briefly to a central interaction in her fiction between what we might call a 'heroine's plot' of romance and a 'hero's plot' of vocation.

' "*The same theme – courtship; and . . . the same catastrophe – marriage*" ' (Jane Eyre, *p. 201*)

It is undeniable that each of Brontë's novels

recapitulates in some form this same basic romance plot that Jane Eyre professes to find of so little significance. It is rather simply summarised: a woman is alone and consequently lonely; she meets and is courted, usually in a strikingly antagonistic way, by a man; external complications intervene and seem to put an end to the relationship; the complications are resolved; marriage, or at least the planning of marriage, ensues. It is in most respects a conventional enough version: heterosexual, exclusive, with marriage as narrative *telos*. But there is more to Brontë's plotting than this. To begin with, set over against this 'female plot' of romance, in one way or another, is what might be called the plot of *Bildung*, of personal ambition and vocation.[49] And then there is a third story: what I should like to call the plot of desire. Now, Nancy Armstrong has argued forcefully that to speak of desire as something that exists before or beyond writing is 'to imbed a modern truth in the referent', and deplores the fact that:

> I find it difficult to think of a single study of the novel that does not posit an opposition between writing and desire in which desire, when written, loses at least some of its individuality, truth, purity, or power, which is nevertheless there for critics to recover.[50]

For Armstrong, though, desire seems to be inextricably linked to sexuality. I want here to use it in a larger sense, as a longing for something (quite probably unformulated) which is different, other, more, than what is available. In this sense, the desire of the woman seems to me to be an important locus of social critique and, sometimes, of envisioned social transformation. Indeed, according to D.A. Miller, it is only some such force that makes narrative possible, for the narratable is precisely that which speaks of desire and so breaks up consensus and the *status quo*: 'the production of narrative – what we called the narratable – is possible only within a logic of insufficiency, disequilibrium, and deferral.'[51] Narrating women as she does, Brontë cannot but place at the centre of her texts the expression of desire as want or need. So, there is a relationship of tension between the plots of romance, of *Bildung* and of desire. And since the plots of romance and of vocation are teleological, while the story of female desire conduces to unimaginable ends, the tension is one between middles and endings, between utopian expansion and socially ratified closure. Where romance charts the reconciliation of the heroine to the already written sexual fate of women, and where *Bildung* plots the reconciliation of self-determination with socialisation, desire can be the name of what is left unaccounted for and undomesticated by these forms of closure.

In the case of *The Professor*, it is primarily the use of her male narrator that allows Brontë to fabricate an apparently harmonious outcome for both romance and vocation. The novel begins, awkwardly, with a letter sent to no-one and nowhere in particular and which receives no response, and this remnant of epistolary form perhaps betrays an uncertainty of address in the usurping of the male voice. But the interposition of the male narrator between the reader and the character of Frances Henri has a particular role in the novel's effacement of desire, for it means that her moments of 'eccentric vigour' (p. 197), 'passionate earnestness' (p. 212) or 'wild vigour' (p. 213) come to us always as spoken for, as already interpreted. They appear in Crimsworth's narrative as momentary flashes of something in excess of his own narrowly-focused and work-aday ambition. So, for instance:

> The display of eccentric vigour never gave her pleasure, and it only sounded in her voice or flashed in her countenance when extraordinary circumstances – and those generally painful – forced it out of the depths where it burned latent. To me, once or twice, she had, in intimate conversation, uttered venturous thoughts in nervous language; but when the hour of such manifestation was past, I could not recall it; it came to itself and of itself departed. (p. 197)

The emphasis here falls, as it must in a first-person narration, upon Crimsworth's interpretations and memories, rather than on what the 'vigour' itself might betoken; as a result, it appears as 'eccentric', 'extraordinary', something incomprehensibly 'of itself'. And for Crimsworth, what is eccentric must be checked or calmed, and consigned to the abyss of repression whence 'I could not recall it.' Nevertheless, such moments serve to unsettle the 'temperate' and 'unostentatious' nature of the desires to which alone he lays claim.

In particular, what is inexplicable about Frances undercuts the way in which romance and vocation are woven together as modes of closure. Although Frances is given something of a fixation on England as her ' "Canaan" ' (p. 145), she is also allowed to show an understanding of the limitations of her promised land, the English school:

> 'In Switzerland I have done but little, learnt but little, and seen but little; my life there was in a circle; I walked the same round every day; I could not get out of it . . .; when I was quite tired of this round, I begged my aunt to go to Brussels; my existence is no larger here, because I am no

richer or higher; I walk in as narrow a limit, but the scene is changed; it would change again if I went to England. I knew something of the bourgeois of Geneva, now I know something of the bourgeois of Brussels; if I went to London, I would know something of the bourgeois of London.' (p. 117)

Similarly, the marriage with Crimsworth leaves her in a state of obscure distress which is never explained:

> Singular to state, she was, or had been crying; when I asked her if she were ready, she said 'Yes, Monsieur,' with something very like a checked sob; . . . I said I was sorry to see her in such low spirits, and requested to be allowed an insight into the origin thereof. She only said, 'It was impossible to help it,' and then voluntarily, though hurriedly, putting her hand into mine, accompanied me out of the room, and ran downstairs with a quick, uncertain step, like one who was eager to get some formidable piece of business over. (p. 203)

Carol Ohmann has remarked that the ending of *The Professor* resolves the tension between the plots of ideal marriage and of economic success into exemplarity,[52] and so it fuses vocation and marriage into one for both protagonists. In this way it seems to shape and restrain the desire of Frances so that it tapers to the closure of the working wife. Even so, Crimsworth's account of their married life focuses disconcertingly on the 'two wives' (p. 207) that she must become in order to provide this form of closure. The extreme disjunction of her two roles betrays that the ending of Frances's plot remains obstinately two endings, and follows the opposed narrative logics of *Bildung* and romance.

By the end of the novel, Crimsworth figures the text's attempt to restrain and keep under surveillance all that threatens the precarious balance of domestic vocation. So it is that the 'kind of electrical ardour and power' which sporadically erupts in the son Victor must be 'if not *whipped* out of him, at least soundly disciplined' (p. 221). Most particularly at stake, though, is the role of Hunsden Yorke Hunsden, whose surrogate, the rabid dog that bears his name, is shot by Crimsworth. It is Hunsden, undomesticated to the end by either vocation or marriage, who is the repository of the wider social world that the Crimsworth closure seeks to deny: with his German metaphysicians and his polyglot discussion, his 'drivelling theorists' and his 'metropolitan, almost . . . cosmopolitan freedom and largeness' (p. 215), Hunsden threatens to unsettle the tableau of the bourgeois family that would otherwise close the novel. And if Hunsden is the unconstrained shadow of Crimsworth, then Frances likewise has her troubling double in the story of the woman who got away, Lucia:

> 'The face is that of one who has made an effort, and a successful and triumphant effort, to wrest some vigorous and valued faculty from insupportable constraint; and when Lucia's faculty got free, I am certain it spread wide pinions and carried her higher than – 'She hesitated.
> 'Than what?' demanded Hunsden.
> 'Than "les convenances" permitted you to follow.'
> (p. 217)

The tale that Frances invents here embodies all the vigorous longing for something more that the novel ultimately seeks to disguise or deny. *The Professor* is, finally, a story of the socialisation of romance and *Bildung* to fit within the usages of *les convenances*. All that would speak of desire is split off and projected, beyond the confines of the novel, onto the unimagined narrative of Lucia.

Jane Eyre, on the other hand, unquestionably and explicitly speaks of its heroine's desire:

> I shall be called discontented. I could not help it: the restlessness was in my nature; it agitated me to pain sometimes. Then my sole relief was to walk along the corridor of the third story, backwards and forwards, safe in the silence and solitude of the spot, and allow my mind's eye to dwell on whatever bright visions rose before it – and certainly they were many and glowing; to let my heart be heaved by the exultant movement which, while it swelled it in trouble, expanded it with life; and best of all to open my inward ear to a tale that was never ended – a tale my imagination created, and narrated continuously; quickened with all of incident, life, fire, feeling, that I desired and had not in my actual existence. (p. 110)

The unending narration of the 'third story' that falls upon Jane's inward ear continually unsettles the teleological, providential narrative that she shares with her readers. And in so doing, it throws into question Jane's insistence on the naturalness and inevitability of the closure of the text in her final calling. The 'restlessness' that at once fuels and enacts this unspoken story is given a kind of serial focus at each point of her picaresque adventures: ambition, passion, vocation, marriage. These focuses in turn resolve themselves into the not unfamiliar trope of the two lovers, the lover of the romance plot (here, Rochester) and the lover of the plot of *Bildung* (here, St John Rivers).

In both these plots, the movement of the novel is governed by an ambivalence which is figured in the repeated shifts from being inside looking out to being outside looking in. Looking is, indeed, a key term in the novel, for this movement of ambivalence is structured around the heroine's attempts to evade the scrutiny and surveillance which threaten to fix her in place, as in the celebrated scene of the double enclosure of the window-seat. But whatever seems to promise expansion proves to offer instead only a new limit to the horizons of Jane's expectations. So, Rochester and his largely unsupervised house, Thornfield Hall, initially provide a space of longing for an unformulated, unembodied utopian future; it is here that Jane's yearning for 'prospects' finds its fullest expression. But the spacious house proves to contain within it a prison for the inarticulate and violent rage of the woman, Bertha. In addition, Rochester as lover is associated with the Gothic, which is on the one hand the mode of 'open horizons, beyond social patterns, rational decision, and institutionally approved emotions',[53] and thus seems to offer a utopian expansion; but it is also, in the words of DuPlessis, 'the form of sexual feudalism'[54] and therefore brings with it closure and restraint.

The arrival of St John Rivers gestures towards a new possibility of the wider life, in the form of religious vocation. That he is literal kin to Jane stresses what is shared between them, and the extent to which he provides an alternative channel of plot for what has been throughout the novel the heroine's own psychic energy and desire. Of course, the missionary story should not be mistaken for a full and present plot of female desire: it constitutes in its way as much of a domestication as the life of secluded marriage that fulfils the plot of romance. But it is noteworthy that, in contrast to *The Professor*, in this novel romance and vocation appear almost until the end to be opposed. It is significant, for example, that Jane definitively rules out marriage with St John:

'I repeat: I freely consent to go with you as your fellow-missionary; but not as your wife: I cannot marry you and become a part of you.' (p. 413)

Although his proposal takes very nearly the form of vocation – 'it was as if I had heard a summons from Heaven' (p. 407) – the space left by that 'as if' permits of refusal. But the telepathic voice of Rochester that wrenches Jane away from one lover to another, one story to another, also quite literally makes of the calling of the wife the vocation of the woman. The ideological dilemma of the Victorian heroine – love without work or work without love – is effaced beneath the language of the calling. At the last, the plot of romance comes to be also the plot of properly womanly vocation: that is, to bear the weight of the (typically feminine) vocation of nurturance and self-subordination which is made possible by the maiming of Rochester. It is the reduced status of Rochester that enables the final dissolution of one form of closure into another. Thereafter it is Rivers, 'full of energy, and zeal, and truth' (p. 457), who takes over as the hero of *Bildung* and whose wholly unironised heroic grandeur at the conclusion provides the ending of Jane's interrupted story of ambition.

The refusals and acceptances of Rochester have often been read as the story of a transformation of romantic relationships, in which Jane comes eventually to marriage only on her own terms of equality. In such a view, during their first period of engagement, she is rendered uneasy by his language of 'angels' and 'fairies' and seeks to establish her full existence in the social world through some form of independence that will not, it is implied, be merely financial:

'It would, indeed, be a relief,' I thought, 'if I had ever so small an independency; I never can bear being dressed like a doll by Mr Rochester, or sitting like a second Danae with the golden shower falling daily around me.' (p. 271)

Her refusal to become 'the successor of these poor girls' (p. 316) the mistresses – ' "often by nature, and always by position, inferior" ' (p. 316), as he now sees them – demonstrates a refusal to surrender self-esteem even to her own passionate impulses. Concomitantly, her decision to return to him even before she knows of Bertha's death suggests that she has learned from her involvement with St John Rivers to see passionate love as itself a value supportive of self-esteem. The resulting marriage, in which 'I am my husband's life as fully as he is mine' (p. 456), marks the adjustment of power between them which alone can guarantee the relationship.

Clearly, there is some appeal in this reading. Nevertheless, if it is to be sustained, it requires coming to terms with the blinding and maiming of Rochester, as well as with the sense of restriction and mutedness that hangs over the Ferndean section of the novel. The first of these has long been regarded as a symbolic castration,[55] and thus either an outburst of vengeful feminism or a sign of sexual timidity. And, in keeping with this view, Jane's accession to financial independence can also be seen to take on a punitive quality: 'feminist, executive, opinionated',[56] suggests Burkhart; the Jane of the ending denies Rochester even the advantage of his wealth. On the other hand, though, a symbolic reading of a different kind has been offered:

We today begin to see that Rochester undergoes, not sexual mutilation as the Freudians claim, but the inevitable suffering necessary when those in power are forced to release some of their power to those who previously had none.[57]

Read as a kind of visionary evocation of transformed relationships between women and men in this way, though, the Ferndean marriage cannot but seem inadequate. As Ohmann puts the case:

> The life Jane and Rochester live together fails . . . to make connection with the social fabric and resonate there. They are no longer sovereign and slave, master and servant; they are citizens, but citizens of a state whose population numbers only two.[58]

But in the marginalisation and confinement of the married pair, as in the maiming and loss that alone makes Rochester marriageable, there is surely some interrogation of the romance plot itself and, more particularly, of the forms of teleology and closure that it brings with it.

One of the many striking oddities of *Shirley* is an apparent contradiction at its very centre. It gives vent to the expression of a desire so radically disruptive that it threatens to overthrow all conventions of linear narrative, and yet, more than any other of Brontë's novels, it ties the desire of women to the plot of romance. An 'impassioned stoicism', in Craik's phrase,[59] and a despairing pessimism pervade the stories of the 'Old Maids' to whom Caroline expects her fate to be linked. The desire which she empathetically attributes to them is formed by the sense of something specifically romantic that is missing:

> Is this enough? Is this to live? Is there not a terrible hollowness, mockery, want, craving, in that existence which is given away to others, for want of something of your own to bestow it on? (p. 174)

In the feminised world of myth and allegory that is

focused upon Shirley, Caroline's form of desire finds its analogue in more rhapsodic vein:

> The girl sat, her body still, her soul astir; occupied, however, rather in feeling than in thinking – in wishing, than hoping, – in imagining, than projecting. . . . Of all things, herself seemed to herself the centre. . . . She asked, was she thus to burn out and perish, her living light doing no good, never seen, never needed, – a star in an else starless firmament, – which nor shepherd, nor wanderer, nor sage, nor priest, tracked as a guide, or read as a prophecy? Could this be, she demanded, when the flame of her intelligence burned so vivid; when her life beat so true, and real, and potent; when something within her stirred disquieted, and restlessly asserted a God-given strength, for which it insisted she should find exercise? (p. 487)

This Eva-Titaness figure finds her fulfilment in the arms of ' "a son of God" ' (p. 489) in a more overtly erotic form of romantic closure than that which befalls, and, we are led to believe, similarly fulfils Caroline.

Of course, sexual desire is in this context metonymic of a wider desire for expansion and transformation of which Rose Yorke, with her claim that ' "I will do more" ' (p. 401), is the chief representative. But her story of doing more cannot be told within the novel – it leads to expulsion from the community, just as the desire of the Luddites for social change causes their transportation. In a novel so passionately committed to its place as *Shirley*, this is surely a telling point. Those who stay on are enabled to do so by the domestication of desire that the closure of the romance plot brings about. The unsatisfactory nature of the marital *telos* is clear, however, in the striking discontinuity between what is said and represented of marriage in the novel and its final invocation as closure. ' "Millions of marriages are unhappy: if everybody confessed the truth, perhaps all are more or less so" ', Helstone tells Caroline (p. 101), and most of what we see suggests that he is right. Whether because of violence, as in the case of Mrs Pryor's marital history, or because of neglect, as in the story of Mary Cave, marriage as a continuing fact within the narrative is scarcely endorsed as a mode of fulfilment. Yet as a form of closure, it nevertheless comes finally to seem not merely the ' "ordinary destiny" ' (p. 174), but also the necessary fulfilment, of women. I shall go on, later, to discuss the importance of ideologies of motherhood in this contradictory resolution, but I want for the moment to focus on the domestication of desire which it enacts.

That domestication is interestingly evident in the relation between Shirley's visionary narrative of the 'bridal-hour of Genius and Humanity' (p. 489) and what might be called the 'ghost' narrative that visits Robert and predicts his eventual marriage with Caroline. The insubstantial Caroline of his visions can be found both in the workplace – ' "But a week ago, I was standing at the top of one of my long rooms, girls were working at the other end, and amongst half a dozen of them, moving to and fro, I seemed to see a figure resembling yours" ' (p. 255) – and in the home: ' "One night, when I came home late from market, I walked into the cottage parlour thinking to find Hortense: but instead of her, I thought I found you" ' (p. 255). In the reduction of Shirley's allegorical visions to Robert's domestic fantasies, we see something of the fate of the feminine in *Shirley*. In both cases, though, the visionary closure must be authorised by the man; just as Shirley's myth-making is scrutinised and marked by Louis Moore, so Caroline's closure depends upon the consent of his brother: ' "I shall not follow you into your mill, Robert, unless you call me there" ' (p. 255). The difference between the two modes, as well as the linked closures that both eventually accede to, are noted for us in the difference between the two brothers. ' "I believe in nothing Utopian" ', declares Robert (p. 495); ' "I . . . believe in Romance" ' (p. 504), says Louis. The refusal of the utopian, here, seems to entail the endorsement of romance.

One reason for this is that the plot of vocation, as it touches upon women, takes so attenuated and pallid a form in this novel. It is transmuted instead into the desperation about under- and unemployment that links social critique in the mythic, rhapsodic vein of the women and in the linear, industrial narrative associated with the world of men. It is not vocation but work that is at stake here. Writing of Scott, D.A. Miller has suggested that:

> The historical novel . . . exists to deprive the course of history, as well as the course of narrative thus motivated, of its necessity . . . [The] entire conflict that has generated the novel must be seen as senseless waste . . . People make history . . . only because people make mistakes: both can and should be avoided.[60]

In much the same way, the desire that drives the narrative of working class dissent in *Shirley* finally emerges as error and waste. The *delirium tremens* that claims the 'half-crazed weaver . . . frantic Antinomian, and . . . mad leveller' Michael Hartley (p. 635) symbolically takes his attempt on the life of Moore and the working-class protest that it represents into the sphere of the irrational, the meaningless. And the

31

transportation of the Luddites involved in the attack on the mill similarly makes of class action criminality. Dissent, whether of workers or of women, is expelled, and stoicism is in both cases transformed into reconciliation under the guidance of paternalism.

Nevertheless, the excess of desire still leaves its traces in the conclusion of the novel. It is there, for example, in that strain of unwritten poetry focused in the heroines which is never fully extinguished by the final conformation to linear historical narrative: 'who shall, of these things, write the chronicle?' (p. 490) is a question that continues to echo unanswered. And the desire for something more, something else, is there too in the train of imagery that binds together the outrage of the 'mad leveller', the rabid dog that perhaps passes on its rage to Shirley, and the vision of the heroine apparently 'fettered to a fixed day . . ., conquered by love, and bound with a vow' (p. 637):

> Pantheress! – beautiful forest-born! – wily, tameless, peerless creature! She gnaws her chain: I see the white teeth working at the steel! She has dreams of her wild woods, and pinings after virgin freedom. (p. 629)

Fettered but wily, dreaming of something other, the panther female surely figures in part the constraint of the text itself.

Villette is notable for what might be called the vicarious nature of its plots; romance and vocation alike are projected away from a heroine whose characteristic quality *as* heroine, as I shall argue below, is virtually the evasion of plotting itself. Both plots are recapitulated, but in the process are subjected to a thoroughgoing and often scornful critique. So, the plot of romance opens the novel, initially given to us in the shape of the quasi-marital relationship of the child Polly and the young

Graham Bretton. Polly is a 'doll' (p. 4), a 'saint' (p. 7), even 'a little Odalisque' (p. 23): a miniaturised compendium of Victorian ideologies of femininity, 'silent, diligent, absorbed, womanly' (p. 11). Her relations with Graham come under explicitly critical scrutiny from the narrator:

> I often wished she would mind herself and be tranquil; but no – herself was forgotten in him; he could not be sufficiently well waited on, nor carefully enough looked after; he was more than the Grand Turk in her estimation. . . . To stand by his knee, and monopolise his talk and notice, was the reward she wanted – not a share of the cake.
>
> With curious readiness did she adapt herself to such schemes as interested him. One would have thought the child had no mind or life of her own, but must necessarily live, move, and have her being in another: now that her father was taken from her, she nestled to Graham, and seemed to feel by his feelings: to exist in his existence. (pp. 18–19)

Later, alone during the school vacation, Lucy establishes a romantic story around the figure of Ginevra:

> By True Love was Ginevra followed: never could she be alone. . . . I imagined her grateful one day to show how much she loved: I pictured her faithful hero half conscious of her coy fondness, and comforted by that consciousness: I conceived an electric chord of sympathy between them, a fine chain of mutual understanding, sustaining communication through a gradual separation of a hundred leagues . . . Ginevra gradually became with me a sort of heroine. (pp. 142–43)

All the elements of the love story are here, and even the capitals of 'True Love' are not enough, given

Brontë's tendency towards capitalised abstractions, to suggest any element of parody at work. And yet this skeleton plot is immediately situated among the narratives of delusion and delirium that shadow Lucy's story:

> One day, perceiving this growing illusion, I said, 'I really believe my nerves are getting overstretched; my mind has suffered somewhat too much; a malady is growing upon it . . . '. (p. 143)

There are a number of such illusory or parodic invocations of romance in *Villette*, among them a series of role-reversals that serve to make unfamiliar what is naturalised by the conventional tropes of romance. This, for example, of Mme Beck:

> Had she, indeed, floating visions of adopting Dr John as a husband, taking him to her well-furnished home, endowing him with her savings, which were said to amount to a moderate competency, and making him comfortable for the rest of his life? (p. 89)

The effect of such sardonic distancing is to throw into question the axiomatic status of the love-plot itself.

Similarly, there are figures and stories of female vocation in the novel: in the various transfigurations of the nun who seems to haunt Lucy, in the actress Vashti whose performance fascinates her and appals her male companion, and in the ambitious Mme Beck whose threatening quality for the narrator derives in part from the combination of a successful working life with having 'no sort of taste for a monastic life' (pp. 418–19). But the plot of *Bildung* is shot through with an ambivalence which finds its focus in the novel's mode of first-person narration. To begin with, ambition and vocation are rather closely associated (in the nun, Père

Silas and Mme Beck, for example) with the Catholic church, and thus, for the truculently Protestant narrator, with what is foreign, devious and intrusive on personal liberty. Yet, though Lucy may despise the 'dread boasts of confessors' (p. 103) who exhort the secrets of women, she nonetheless hears the 'voluntary confession' of Ginevra Fanshawe (p. 78); and although she feels 'no particular vocation to undertake the surveillance of ethereal creatures' (p. 110), it is a role into which her narration often casts her.

Bildung and romance are played off against one another in such a way as to suggest the inadequacy of either and the apparent narrative incompatibility of the two. For the most part, Lucy's own particular plot of romance, unconventional as it is, is used to motivate and enable the plot of *Bildung*: it is M. Paul who threatens, cajoles and bullies Lucy through her education and he who provides the school that stands in the place of the marital home as the end of romance. The ending of the novel, with its sudden swerve away from the *telos* of marriage, may appear to privilege vocation, or at least the life of work, over romance. The conclusion of *Villette* has sometimes been seen as a kind of recognition of the guilty fantasy of allowing a heroine love and independence at once:

> The combination of love and quest, of autonomy and subordination, of being what a woman should be and of being more, was simply too good to be true; it was a private fantasy, worked out in isolation from the forces of the larger world, and, finally, Brontë knew it.[61]

In this, I suppose, one might contrast it with the ending of *Jane Eyre*. And yet, it seems to me that *Villette* is not teleological at all; other than the necessary survival of its first-person narrator, the novel effectively offers no conclusion for her at all. Instead, and as if to highlight this, we are given two versions of a 'happy ending'. First, we have a hypothetical ending in the 'sunny imaginations' of certain implied readers with whom actual readers are discouraged from identifying by the use of the third-person rather than the second-person form:

> Let it be theirs to conceive the delight of joy born again fresh out of great terror, the rapture of rescue from peril, the wondrous reprieve from dread, the fruition of return. Let them picture union and a happy succeeding life. (p. 451)

The other conclusion, immediately following, belongs to the mode of *Bildung* and also to the stories of others:

> Madame Beck prospered all the days of her life; so did Père Silas; Madame Walravens fufilled her ninetieth year before she died. (p. 451)

These, then, are the fitting conclusions of the teleological stories of love and vocation, but the heroine herself comes to rest in neither of them. ' "I have my sort of life apart from yours" ', she tells Paulina earlier in the novel (p. 387), and the recognition of this 'sort of life' that cannot be figured in the narratives of woman is the most radical gesture of the text. Ultimately, the desire that drives *Villette* takes a different form from that of any other of the Brontë novels. It shapes itself as a sceptical interrogation of the very nature of plotting, and resides in the refusal to accede to the conventionalised modes of closure of the narrated woman.

Although Charlotte Brontë's writing has only sporadically the visionary quality of her sister Emily's *Wuthering Heights*, I think it is nevertheless possible to say of it what Leo Bersani has said of visionary literature in general: that, often, 'it expresses the anguish of unfulfilled desire, but that anguish carries within it the stubborn belief that visionary desires *could* be fulfilled.'[62] Anguish is not far to seek in Brontë's heroines, of course. But in the occasional 'eccentric vigour' of Frances Henri, in Jane Eyre's sequestered marriage to a sightless husband, in the fettered and pining panther of Shirley Keeldar, and in the untold history of Lucy Snowe, there still resides a core of utopian desire, of critique of the very plots that make closure possible. However much the stories that tell us woman may repeat themselves, we are constantly reminded by the self-conscious and mistrustful mode of her plotting that things might still be otherwise.

Chapter One

The Professor

'I like unexaggerated intercourse'[1]

The Professor's is a world of doubleness. Virtually every major character is radically divided: William himself hears 'two voices within me' (p. 22); Frances, always potentially both the ' "lady-abbess" ' and the ' "Swiss sibyl' " (p. 195), becomes at last 'two wives' (p. 207) to William; Hunsden's palindromic name draws attention to the various ambivalences and ambiguities he seems to embody for the narrator. Pelet and Zoraïde are more simply duplicitous, and the 'plague-spot of dissimulation' (p. 81) similarly marks almost all the pupils with whom William has to do. That is to say, many of the characters are professors, manifesting one motive, feeling or state of mind but also privately harbouring another. That 'other' is discoverable by unwearying surveillance – as Edward uses 'prowling and prying' in an attempt to break through his brother's equally watchful 'lynx-eyes' of caution (p. 22) – and by skilled reading:

I showed him my countenance with the confidence that
one would show an unlearned man a letter written in
Greek; he might see lines, and trace character[s], but he
could make nothing of them; my nature was not his
nature, and its signs were to him like the words of an
unknown tongue. (p. 14)

These 'signs', like the 'plague-spot' of the pupils, are
among the ways in which the body is represented, in
this novel, as a text that incarnates a truth of character.
No amount of duplicity can altogether erase this text,
but it can be misread or overlooked. As the simile of the
'unlearned man' and Greek which the Eton-educated
William employs suggests, the reading and proper
interpretation of such a text depends upon the acquisition of a set of reading skills. William's deployment of
interpretive strategies can be seen, here as elsewhere
in Brontë, in the pseudo-science of phrenology,
reinforced by the conventions of physiognomy. They
emerge in a form so extreme as to border on the absurd
in William's reading of the girl from the '– Islands',
Juanna Trista:

I wonder that any one, looking at that girl's head and
countenance, would have received her under their roof.
She had precisely the same shape of skull as Pope Alexander the Sixth . . . narrow as was her brow, it presented
space enough for the legible graving of two words, Mutiny
and Hate; in some one of her other lineaments – I think the
eye – cowardice had also its distinct cipher. (p. 80)

Frances, too, engages in a form of such activity. On the
basis of Hunsden's portrait of his lost love, Lucia, she is
able to 'read' a whole narrative:

'I am sure Lucia once wore chains and broke them . . . .
The face is that of one who has made an effort, and a

successful and triumphant effort, to wrest some vigorous
and valued faculty from insupportable constraint.' (p. 217)

The legible body then becomes a fundamental text in
the struggles for self-protection and mastery that
characterise relationship in this novel: for example,
Zoraïde's eyebrows (p. 74) and Frances's smile (p. 101)
in their different ways serve to provide an access –
indisputable because somatic – to the unprotected,
unprofessional self. To be a legible text, here, always
brings with it the threat of possible mastery by
another, and so a basic tactic of survival is to conceal
the body. Hence Crimsworth's armour, the 'casque
with the visor down' (p. 14) or the 'breast-plate of
steely indifference' (p. 68). And hence, more strikingly,
the fact that the 'four pictures' (only three of them
described, in any case) which William uses to convey to
the reader the different phases of his life are all
unpopulated landscapes from which his own
potentially legible body is absent. That he is a 'professor' in his narratorial relationship to his reader
becomes momentarily clear at that point.

Any opening of or onto the self renders one vulnerable in struggle. The language of walking, treading,
climbing, which is so prominent in the novel functions
partly as a continuing allusion to the thoroughly de-
spiritualised version of *The Pilgrim's Progress* that
structures the overt self-help ideology of the book; but
is also conveys something of this sense of interrelation-
ship as somatised power struggle:

> me, [Zoraïde] still watched, still tried by the most
> ingenious feats – she roved round me, baffled, yet
> persevering; I believe she thought I was like a smooth and
> bare precipice, which offered neither jutting stone or tree-
> root, nor tuft of grass to aid the climber. (p. 84)

If Zoraïde were able to gain a foothold, she would, as we continue to say, walk all over him:

> 'I am mistaken if she will not yet leave the print of her stealing steps on thy heart, Crimsworth.'
> 'Of her steps? Confound it, no! My heart is not a plank to be walked on.' (p. 75)

If the body serves, then, as a dangerous agent of betrayal, then clearly sexual desire brings with it much risk. It brings the struggle for mastery within:

> There are impulses we can control; but there are others which control us, because they attain us with a tiger-leap, and are our masters ere we have seen them. (p. 184)

William's understanding of sexuality is at once oblique and pervasive; his is a world of voyeurism and sexual paranoia. Sexual threats and rivals are everywhere, though the narrator himself is apt to attribute this sexualisation of the universe to the baneful influence of the Catholic church. No woman – young, old, committed elsewhere – can fail to have designs upon William's body, it seems. Even Hypochondria appears to him as 'a dreaded and ghastly concubine' (p. 190). Brontë gives a comic account of such male sexual fears in William's response to an invitation to tea on the part of Zoraïde's elderly mother:

> 'Surely she's not going to make love to me,' said I. 'I've heard of old Frenchwomen doing odd things in that line; and the goûter? They generally begin such affairs with eating and drinking, I believe . . .'
> Gracious heavens! The first view of her seemed to confirm my worst apprehensions. There she sat, dressed out in a light green muslin gown, on her head a lace cap with flourishing red roses in her frill; her table was carefully spread; there were fruit, cakes, and coffee, with a

bottle of something – I did not know what. Already the
cold sweat started on my brow, already I glanced back over
my shoulder at the closed door . . . . (p. 56)

A rare moment of retrospective self-irony is allowed to
the narrator here, but the assumption that sexual
desire and activity are literally foreign – 'odd things'
liable to be done by 'Frenchwomen' – is one that
persists in his narration. It is, after all, desire that
threatens to turn him into an 'Oriental' (p. 8), a 'pasha'
(p. 151), a participant in a 'modern French novel'
(p. 154).[2] One of the ways in which Frances resolves
William's dilemmas is by bringing together the 'recluse,
rather conventual' look (p. 194) slightly oddly
associated with her English Protestantism and the
moments of 'wild vigour' when 'her glance [is] so
thrilling and ardent – her action so rapid and strong'
(p. 213). Within their relationship, French is the
language of erotic flirtation:

> Talk French to me she would, and many a punishment she
> has had for her wilfulness. I fear the choice of chastise-
> ment must have been injudicious, for instead of correcting
> the fault, it seemed to encourage its renewal. (p. 209)

English, on the other hand – and especially, it seems,
Wordsworth's English – is the language of 'penance' of
the 'submissive and supplicating little mortal woman'
(p. 210) whose deference allows William's reassertion
of superiority. It is because 'our desires were temperate' (p. 213) that William's self-control remains vigilant
and that this maintenance of role remains within his
control.

Sex poses a multiple threat to William, because it
jeopardises self-mastery and throws into instability the
roles of mastering and mastered. At moments, there

seems to be an equation between control of the body and a larger sense of integrity that is more commonly associated, in nineteenth-century fiction, with women.[3] In the episode of the invitation to tea, he undergoes a fantasy of rape-seduction far more fearful and explicit than anything Brontë assigns to her female characters.[4] One of the uses of the male narrator is precisely to allow more open discussion of such 'improper' topics. In addition to this fear, however, it is possible to see in William moments of anxiety about performance and it is perhaps not wholly fanciful to see this in terms of sexual 'performance'. After all, following much peeping and peering through cracks and windows, he undergoes something of a sexual initiation on his entry to the world of women that is Zoraïde's school.[5] Zoraïde – whose cheek reminds him of 'the bloom of a good apple' (p. 62) – is frequently associated with gardens; indeed, his first meeting with her gives him his 'first glimpse of *the* garden' (p. 60; Brontë's italics), and she opens to him the 'enclosed demesne which had hitherto been an unknown region' (p. 61). It is she who ushers him through the 'great folding-doors' that separate him from the mysteries of femaleness (p. 65). Arriving for his first performance as a professor among women, he nervously handles his 'thick crayon of white chalk' and 'finger[s] the sponge in order to ascertain that it was in a right state of moisture' (p. 65) before proceeding to his duty – a duty initially executed with so little authority that it provokes the girls to laughter: 'c'est un véritable blanc-bec' (p. 66). William has sometimes struck critics of the novel as androgynous,[6] but he is surely nowhere more so than in the combination of sexual fears and anxieties that Brontë gives him.

That his visit from a succubus-like Hypochondria should follow so closely upon the moment when 'my desires, folding wings, weary with long flight, had just alighted on the very lap of fruition' (p. 190) is perhaps not as opaquely astonishing to the reader as it is to the narrator. This visitation from a 'nightmarish personification of female sexuality',[7] materialising after Frances has been restored to him, as if by magic, at the graveside in the cemetery with its ever-open gates, makes manifest the connection the novel establishes between melancholy and desire, bodily need and death.[8] The body brings with it a double anguish of self-betrayal and death, both of them enforced recognitions of the limits of control in this narrative of self-making and mastery.

The making of a man

The Professor comes close, in the outline of its plot at least, to the classic form of the *Bildungsroman*: a young hero turns his back on the society that has produced him but now trammels his abilities and desires, and finds a form of meaningful self-assertion in the social world elsewhere. Brontë's Preface rather urgently proclaims the 'plain and homely' nature of the narrative, and the element of striving that she wishes to make central in her plot:

> I said to myself that my hero should work his way through life as I had seen real living men work theirs – that he should never get a shilling he had not earned – that no sudden turns should lift him in a moment to wealth and high station; that whatever small competency he might gain, should be won by the sweat of his brow. (p. xxiii)

This overt commitment to self-help and individual initiative is somewhat undermined, though, by the thoroughgoing contingency in William's story that serves to free him from all responsibility, either for his acts or for his character. Not he but his brother dictates the hostile terms of their relationship; not he but Hunsden initiates the break with the brother and the departure for Belgium; not he but Mme Reuter brings about access to that ' "Eden" ' (p. 59), the girls' school; not he but Zoraïde and Pelet determine that she is not a suitable partner for him; not he but Zoraïde turns him into a 'pasha' (p. 151); not he but the lumpish Belgians turn him into a 'despot' (p. 53); not he but Frances insists that she call him 'Monsieur', after their marriage as before; even the killing of his son Victor's dog is a deed of 'stern necessity' (p. 219). It is chance that puts the drowning Vandenhuten boy before his eyes; and chance – after his attempt at self-help in tracking Frances through the Protestant churches of Brussels has failed – that brings him to the graveyard where she stands. Most important among the instigators, surely, is Hunsden. William may wish to become Providence in the life of Frances (p. 187), but Hunsden unequivocally plays such a role in his life, becoming an unusually visible plot-manipulator, what has been called a 'narrator-in-disguise'.[9] But as William's narration becomes compulsively a tale of self-making, Hunsden becomes the repository of all that this carefully self-constructed Professor can no longer accommodate: of an aristocratic connection he has ostensibly cast off, of a homoeroticism his marriage suppresses (or triangulates), of a political activism betrayed by the transformation of the language of revolt into the principles of personal advancement, of a social world that threatens to unsettle the precarious achievements of personal and professional power. William's shooting of the dog that bears Hunsden's name, and that William declares rabid, is only partially successful as an exorcism of those betrayals and suppressions, for even afterwards Hunsden's influence over the son Victor persists. It is acknowledged in a sentence where the convention of writing-to-the-moment takes on the hallucinatory quality of a psychic haunting:

> I see him now; he stands by Hunsden, who is seated on the lawn under the beech; Hunsden's hand rests on the boy's collar, and he is instilling God knows what principles into his ear. (p. 221)

Dianne Sadoff has noted the 'self-fathering' nature of William's autobiography,[10] and certainly the third reprise of Oedipal narrative that focuses on Victor emphasises William's troubled supremacy in the place of the father.[11] Doubly in possession of the mother – that is, once as victorious son, in the form of the portrait that is characteristically won for him by Hunsden, and once as victorious father, in the form of the person of Frances – he has by the end of the novel assumed the role of the patriarchally powerfully male. In the name of the son, Victor, surely lies a suggestion of the jealous insecurity with which he occupies such a place. Franco Moretti has characterised the *Bildungsroman* as the form by which we seek to resolve 'a dilemma conterminous with modern bourgeois civilization: the conflict between the ideal of *self-determination* and the equally imperious demands of *socialization*.'[12] In the case of *The Professor*, those imperatives are strikingly intertwined. In the course of the novel, interestingly, William becomes all those things that, precisely, he once claimed not to be: 'I am no Oriental' (p. 8), but now, having become 'barbarous as a pasha' (p. 151), he ends in possession of 'two wives' (p. 207); 'I am not a professor' (p. 46), but now he has both the professional status and the tone of self-proclaiming that that term implies; 'I was no Pope' (p. 154), but by the end he exercises the authority and presumes the ex cathedral status of the father in the treatment of his son. *The Professor* is, as Eagleton comments, a story of 'classic bourgeois progress',[13] but intertwined with and potentiating that story of self-making throughout is also a tale of socialisation: of becoming masculine. And, as such, the novel raises vital questions about the interrelations, social and ideological, of gender and power.

Like a male Jane Eyre, perhaps, William Crimsworth executes an exemplary progress from powerlessness to mastery. And like that other outlaw from patrilineage, Heathcliff, he begins orphaned and oppressed and ends – save for the unsettling presence of Hunsden – in possession of all that once excluded him. The female fairy-tale motif of Cinderella has been remarked elsewhere in Brontë's fiction, and it applies equally to William, although role-reversal does not extend so far as to allow Frances the transformative power of Prince Charming. William's story draws, indeed, on tropes of plot victimage more commonly associated with female protagonists: resisting being forcibly married off by a wicked uncle, treated like a drudge by a malicious sibling, left to look on at the ball like a Cinderella-governess, nearly the victim of rape/seduction.[14] It is noticeable that an instability of sex characterises both William and Hunsden, at least in the earlier part of the novel. Hunsden's writing, for example, is 'neither masculine nor exactly feminine' (p. 158). He has 'small, and even feminine, . . . lineaments' but a 'powerful and massive' presence (p. 25); more oddly, surely, he has 'now the mien of a morose bull, and anon that of an arch and mischievous girl' (p. 26). He in turn sees William as a transmogrification of 'Rebecca on a camel's hump, with bracelets on her arms and a ring in her nose' (p. 23) – and thus himself something of a mixture of woman and bull. Interestingly, although in William's case this admixture of the female serves sometimes to connect powerlessness with femininity, in the case of Hunsden there is no such implication. Hunsden, rather, conforms from the first to some of the stereotypes of masculinity: in his sadistic manipulation of William's emotions, in his tyrannical self-assertion, in his social power in the world.

Some feminist readings of the novel have suggested that the connection of William's initial powerlessness with feminisation, and the occasional shifts of role in the master/slave relationship with Frances, indicate that gender has been productively prised apart from sex and aligned, instead, with power. Moglen, for instance, argues that:

> Brontë has begun to reject . . . an exclusively biological definition of femininity. To some extent, she begins to see femininity as an existential condition, determined by psychological and social forces. To be powerless, without social, economic, or legal status; to be unconfident, dependent, insecure, and vulnerable – is to be female. So much is clear.[15]

It seems to me, though, that although *The Professor* raises and challenges certain stereotypes of gender – in Mrs Edward Crimsworth as child-bride, in the rumbustious and sexually aware girls of Zoraïde's

school, in Frances's refusal to be a ' "patient Grizzle" '
(p. 212), in Hunsden's delicacy and asceticism – in ways
that are sometimes quite brutal, at the same time it also
restates other gender stereotypes in equally disturbing
ways. This is, I think, related to the lack of access to
any woman's consciousness – a lack unique in Brontë's
adult fiction – other than as refracted through the male
narrator. William's narration of himself and of women
is shaped and shadowed by the acquisition of a masculinity that is not naturalised as intrinsic; it is as factitious
as the armour on which the novel so often draws for
images of self-protection.

William, that is to say, learns his masculinity as a
crucial part of his social progress; he is not only a *self-
made* man, but also a self-made *man*. Gilbert and Gubar
suggest that *The Professor* offers a 'chilling vision of the
male world',[16] and certainly, imagining for herself a
male narrator, Brontë imagines misogyny, prurience,
and barely repressed violence. It is a harsh world in
which relationships of all kinds – family, friendship,
shared work, love – take the form and language of
competition and power struggle. Initially, William's
position amidst the unmotivated hostility, unforgiving
rancour and contemptuous patronage of his male
acquaintance is one of a relative powerlessness and
passivity. But at a vital moment Hunsden points out
the possible interpretations and limitations of meek-
ness:

'If you are patient because you expect to make something
eventually out of Crimsworth, notwithstanding his tyr-
anny, or perhaps by means of it, you are what the world
calls an interested and mercenary, but it may be a very
wise fellow; if you are patient because you think it a duty
to meet insult with submission, you are an essential sap,

and in no shape the man for my money; if you are patient because your nature is phlegmatic, flat, inexcitable, and that you cannot get up to the pitch of resistance, why, God made you to be crushed; and lie down by all means, and lie flat, and let Juggernaut ride well over you.' (p. 27)

Hunsden's advice, with its gendered implications (a 'fellow', a 'man', the erectile imagery of 'getting up' to resistance), shapes William's account of his progress thereafter, and it brings out clearly the ideological implications of the 'self-help' rhetoric which the book, and the Preface, employ. Those implications are simple: not to resist is to be complicit, and to be complicit is to be responsible. The oppressed are oppressed because they choose to be so.

William draws from this the lesson that the revolted slave must seek to be the master, and it is on this basis that all his relationships are represented thereafter. So, the 'showers of Brabant saliva and handfuls of Low Country mud' (p. 53) which greet any indulgence on his part turn him, reciprocally, into a 'despot' (p. 53). Friendships with Pelet and Zoraïde are conducted on the basis of self-protective wariness and mutual surveillance. Sexual desire only provides the occasion and the means of further struggles for power. The William who initially seeks a 'Promethean spark' (p. 8) of intellectual sympathy in women later acts out an entirely different relation to it; Zoraïde's undoubted intelligence having proved, for him, merely another weapon in her armoury for the subjugation of men, he punishes her with the tale of an unrequited passion that serves to exalt him and to abase her. Women here are fascinated by ill-treatment, bewitched by coldness, captivated by rejection; the traits of the slave confirm, even engender, those of the master:

I had ever hated a tyrant; and, behold, the possession of a slave, self-given, went near to transform me into what I abhorred! There was at once a sort of low gratification in receiving this luscious incense from an attractive and still young worshipper; and an irritating sense of degradation in the very experience of the pleasure. When she stole about me with the soft step of a slave, I felt at once barbarous and sensual as a pasha. (p. 151)

Nor is this peculiar to Zoraïde, it must be noted. Frances shares these same traits, and her relation with William is, as Eagleton puts it, 'transparently sado-masochistic',[17] featuring prominently the language of check and punishment eagerly sought, of mastery and submission voluntarily granted:

For I had ever remarked, that however sad or harassed her countenance might be when I entered a room, yet after I had been near her, spoken to her a few words, given her some directions, uttered perhaps some reproofs, she would, all at once, nestle into a nook of happiness, and look up serene and revived. The reproofs suited her best of all. (p. 145)

It is true that, as Kucich has remarked,[18] there are moments of instability and reversal in William's relationships. The pasha-like master, for instance, is accompanied by a 'degradation' that reintroduces the role of the slave (p. 151), and the paragraph dealing with Frances which I have quoted above is soon followed by the comment that 'she made me in a fashion (though happily she did not know it) her subject if not her slave' (p. 146).

However, I do not think, as one might go on to deduce from Kucich's analysis of the master/slave couple, that what emerges from this is a thoroughgoing realignment of gender roles with power and powerlessness. One reason why William must learn to be a 'man' is that love is no protected haven beyond the reach of power; the domestic or personal sphere is, clearly, as fully social as the workplace. And one reason for this, in turn, is the extent to which the novel represents women and men alike as bound to their gender roles by pleasure, by the 'low gratification' of the master and the 'nook of happiness' of the slave. This emerges most obviously in the figure of Frances Henri. The androgyny hinted at in her name produces, in the end, two different Franceses for her two different roles. By day, at work, she is competent and self-reliant, a 'stately and elegant woman' with 'much anxious thought on her large brow' (p. 207); by night, as wife, she is 'like a child and a novice' (p. 210), dependent and adoring. The striving for independence and equality in the area of work and earning capacity that the novel allows her is set against the delights of willing submission in intimate relationship. The courtship and marriage of William and Frances are imbued with none of the sense of the erotic power of wit that grants Jane Eyre or Lucy Snowe at least a discursive equality with their 'master' lovers, and the use of the male narrator gives us only a simple and indirect account of the woman's relation to this voluntary self-subjection. As a result, the extremes of domination and submission emerge more starkly in this novel than they will elsewhere in the fiction. Nevertheless, the continuing importance of loving and being loved to Brontë's oppressed heroines will raise again and again those important and still unresolved issues about the implication of gender and pleasure in one another that are, perhaps, rather baldly stated in *The Professor*.

Mastering language

William Crimsworth seems to share what are often identified as the most typical traits of the Brontë heroines: orphaned, repressed, displaced, victimised. And yet: it seems that the very fact of his being a male character turns them from the outset into something else. He is not simply an orphan, he is a self-made man. His repression is imaged in the wearing of armour, which is a form not only of self-protection, after all, but also of militancy. And when victimage and vulnerability *are* dwelt upon, the recurring image and self-image of him as Israelite in Egypt bring with them, together with the sense of exile, also a sense of being chosen.[19] All that is more radically orphaned and unprotected belongs instead to Frances Henri, whose doubled androgynous name suggests her relation to Crimsworth of double – ' "Wilhelmina Crimsworth" ' (p. 191) – as well as lover.

Frances, as has been pointed out in differing critical contexts from the political to the psychological, projects and resolves the conflicts and paradoxes of William and his situation: she reconciles the familiar and the foreign, Crimsworth's conservatism and Hunsden's radicalism, passivity and activity, the roles of the teacher and the pupil, the domestic and the professional.[20] But the resolution she effects for him takes for her the peculiar form, overdetermined by gender, of fragmentation: 'I seemed to possess two wives', says William (p. 207). The reconciliation of the opposing needs of the male characters splits apart those of the female. Her professional freedom is obtained only by means of personal submission,[21] and only the development of a 'schizophrenic personality'[22] enables her to perform adequately in the roles of both wife-and-mother and headmistress. William, for all Brontë's prefatory insistence on 'the sweat of his brow' (p. xxiii) and individual striving, can rely at crucial moments on his birthright of gender and class. At times he shares with Lucy Snowe, in *Villette*, the sense of being all at sea, borne along by the tide in an enforced passivity. At the low point of his financial and emotional fortunes, for example, he feels this:

> At that hour my bark hung on the topmost curl of a wave of fate, and I knew not on what shoal the onward rush of the billow might hurl it. (p. 177)

But where Lucy's story will be for ever foundering in storm and shipwreck, William is able to draw upon the resources of his gentleman's education: 'I had not been brought up at Eton and boated and bathed and swam there ten long years for nothing' (p. 162), after all, for it is that that makes possible the rescue from drowning of the Vandenhuten boy that changes the course of his life. Frances, by contrast, has no such class- and gender-specific good fortune, unless, of course, we are to argue, with Brontë, for the exceptional luck of having been 'born an Englishwoman, and reared up Protestant' (p. 87). Frances is without a birthright; indeed, as her *devoir* on the subject of Alfred and the burned cakes suggests, when she comes to envisage the possibility of such a thing as birthright, she begins by positing a male consciousness.

Frances's inheritances are scant: a dual allegiance of patriotism, a tea-service, a few books, and a ' "mother tongue" ' (p. 113) that has been lost and can only be restored to her by the offices of a male teacher. Like Jane Eyre, who paints, and the silent female poets of *Shirley*, Frances is an artist. But the very means by which she achieves that status is problematically linked with her sex, because of her dependence upon the enabling intervention of the man. And her 'Jane' poem establishes a further, and again highly problematic, link between the 'woman' and the 'writer' in this woman writer:

> The strong pulse of Ambition struck
> In every vein I owned;
> At the same instant, bleeding, broke
> A secret, inward wound.
>
> (p. 183)

This stanza sets up an undecidable opposition between the menstrual image which posits a fertile simultaneity between ambition and femaleness, and the alternative linking of ambition and haemorrhage, debilitating loss. The 'Jane' of the poem has learned what is to be learned from *her* Professor, but the 'triumph' (p. 183) which mastery of language brings her co-exists with the 'sorrow' (p. 183) of the relinquishing of love that appears consequent upon it. Frances's own solution, however, will follow a different course.

Zoraïde Reuter, echoing the terms of Southey's famously discouraging letter to Brontë,[23] opposes aspirations toward writing in women:

> 'It appears to me that ambition, *literary* ambition especially, is not a feeling to be cherished in the mind of a woman: would not Mdlle Henri be much safer and happier if taught to believe that in the quiet discharge of social duties consists her real vocation, than if stimulated to aspire after applause and publicity?' (p. 123)

In its immediate context, and certainly in a first reading, William's reply would seem to be an ironic one:

> 'Indisputably, Mademoiselle,' was my answer. 'Your opi-

nion admits of no doubt'; and, fearful of the harangue being renewed, I retreated under cover of that cordial sentence of assent. (p. 123)

However, the novel overall shows just the course of events that Zoraïde Reuter has prescribed. Frances Henri's *'literary* ambition' proves only a means towards the 'quiet discharge of social duties' as William's wife and colleague. Nor has her writing much to do with any expectation of 'applause and publicity'; it comes to us only through the medium of her teacher/lover. Her *devoirs* are sternly criticised, ignored and treated as the disguised expression of personal feeling. Her only 'public readings' are in fact solitary performances, and their reproduction for the reader depends upon William's having eavesdropped or stolen her paper. Her very language comes from him; only he can restore to her the ' "mother tongue" ' (p. 113) that enables her to use the 'language of her own heart' (p. 179). As woman writer, Frances is available to the reader only through the forcible intervention of the man: 'I installed myself in her place, allowing her to stand deferentially at my side' (p. 122). Gilbert and Gubar argue that William comes 'to incarnate a male literary tradition that discourages female writers',[24] but this is, I think, too simple a statement of the case. It is, after all, Zoraïde who argues for discouragement, while William also provides the means and an audience for her writing. What is at stake here, it seems to me, is rather a relation of control and censorship than of outright discouragement. The novel's exploration of likeness between Crimsworth and Frances is predicated upon a keen awareness of differential relations of power, and not least in the power that belongs to the mastery of language. The woman, here, may write only when empowered by the man.

Nonetheless, if this is what *The Professor* professes, still its very existence and availability testify to another possibility. Brontë, defying the advice of Southey, continued to write. What is more, she emulates and inverts William's theft and publication of Frances's words by 'stealing' the words of Southey and giving them to us in the mouth of another woman, albeit an 'agent of patriarchy'.[25] And finally, she persisted, in the face of at least six rejections by (male) publishers in her wish and attempts to get *The Professor* published. It is, I suppose, only an irony of history that its eventual appearance in print was posthumous and had to be authorised by her husband, installed in 'her place' at Haworth:

> It has been represented to me that I ought not to withhold 'The Professor' from the public. I have therefore consented to its publication.
>
> A.B. Nicholls
>
> HAWORTH PARSONAGE
> *September 22nd, 1856*
>
> (p. xxiv)

Chapter Two

Jane Eyre

Ginger-nuts

Counselling the young Jane Eyre in the avoidance of going to Hell, the Reverend Mr Brocklehurst tells her an anecdote:

> 'I have a little boy, younger than you, who knows six Psalms by heart; and when you ask him which he would rather have, a gingerbread-nut to eat, or a verse of a Psalm to learn, he says: "Oh! the verse of a Psalm! Angels sing Psalms;" says he, "I wish to be a little angel here below;" he then gets two nuts in recompense for his infant piety.'[1]

This story passes without comment, other than Jane's infant impiety that ' "Psalms are not interesting" ', and it is hard to know who, if anyone, is being ironised here: Mr Brocklehurst, with his stupendous obliviousness to manipulation, seems the most obvious candidate. But this fable of deferred gratification rehearses in little, and with the same puzzling apparent lack of self-consciousness, the path that Jane herself will follow in the course of her narrative, a course which leads her quite flagrantly into the best of both worlds, into material wealth and spiritual capital, into the satisfaction of appetite and the self-satisfaction of sacrifice. Jane, of course, has somewhat clearer notions of the proper sphere for angels than the pious infant, and indeed than Rochester, who appears to think they are interchangeable with witches and fairies, and are to be had in the house as mistresses, if not wives: ' "I am no angel", she tells him, "and I will not be one till I die" ' (p. 262). Nevertheless, Providence, like Mr Brocklehurst, rewards her choice of principle over pleasure with plenty of gingerbread, lavishly gilded. What has troubled many readings of the novel has been precisely this coincidence of the narrating and narrated Janes, the sense that no textual space is left for consideration of the way in which the oppressed and rebellious child turns into the lady, the victim of the Red Room into the keeper of the keys in the patriarchal household. One longstanding answer to the problem has been to refer it back to Brontë herself, to deplore a lapse into 'wish-fulfilment' which can, as often as not, be in its turn attributed to the author's marital and sexual status at the time of composition: 'the invention of a thirty-year old virgin' as one commentator succinctly, if offensively, puts it.[2] Alternatively, some have attributed some level of disguised motivation to the character herself, taking the 'providence' of the narrative less as divine intervention than as foresight, prudent and timely care for the future: so, Eagleton finds 'a good deal of dexterous calculation' in Jane's pursuit of Mr Rochester's money.[3]

The problem of the unremarked ideological shift in the novel becomes acute, of course, in feminist readings, and there has developed something of a dichotomy. On the one hand, more narrowly class- and race-blind interpretations have celebrated here a feminist version of what Hermione Lee calls an 'epic of self-determination':[4] the painful acquisition of identity (' "I am Jane Eyre" ' (p. 439)), of independence (' "I am independent, sir, as well as rich: I am my own mistress" ' (p. 440)), and of a marriage of equals ('I am my husband's life as fully as he is mine' (p. 456)). This reading, focusing on the realist level of the narrative – a persecuted orphan, a rebellious girl, a woman finding satisfaction in education and work, a female narrator finding the language to tell her own story – in the process also takes on, in Gayatri Spivak's words, 'the mesmerizing focus of the "subject-constitution" of the female individualist'[5] that has so often been the tale feminist criticism tells itself. On the other hand, if the focus is adjusted to take in those marginalised but constitutive textual discourses of class and race, another story emerges: 'no social revolutionary', argues Lee R. Edwards, 'Jane is rather a displaced spiritual aristocrat'; Politi analyses how 'the narrative together with the girl-child will grow from revolted marginality to quiescent socialisation, reblending the contradictions which it initially exposed, thus securing its survival through the convention of a "happy ending" '; and Weissman concludes that 'the end of the book reveals the first half for what it is – not the rage of the Romantic radical who wants justice, but the rage of the outsider who just wants to get in.'[6]

Most tellingly, perhaps, our attention is then drawn to those other women whose stories are occluded by Jane's: for example, to Bessie, female servant whose tales and ballads are Jane's alternative education, in

orphanhood, in class position, and in narrating; to
Grace Poole, working-class woman who guards the
secrets of female delinquency and 'giant propensities'
(p. 310) in the heart of the 'gentleman's manor-house'
(p. 100); and, above all, to Bertha Mason Rochester.[7]
Bertha: not only madwoman in the attic,[8] after all, but
also skeleton in the closet, the 'dark' secret, the maddening burden of imperialism concealed in the heart of
every English gentleman's house of the time. Dark, but
not black: while the word 'creole' marks a double
displacement of origins, Bertha is fixed as white by her
status as daughter of settler planters. Maddening, but
not maddened: the intrinsic, racial/familial nature of
Bertha's 'moral madness'[9] serves to exculpate Rochester, and with him the English gentry class, from so
much as complicity in her plight.

Jane Eyre, like many another Victorian novel, turns
upon questions of inheritance, but here in an unusually
multiple and self-mirroring form. Every main character
in the novel is involved in a series of inheritances
diverted and denied, and each of these is restored by
the end of the book. Most importantly for my purposes
here, all of them derive from Jamaica and from Bertha's
blood relations, that same blood that is 'tainted' with
madness and vice. Here, you might say, lies the source
of the ginger for Jane's ginger-nuts. Through Uncle
Eyre's connection with the planter family, the Masons,
this inheritance links Jane into the financial chain that
ultimately binds together the military (Diana's naval
husband), the clergy (Mary's clergyman husband) and
the cultural imperialism of St John Rivers, who will use
his share of the inheritance to 'labour for his race'
(p. 457) in India. Most obviously, Jamaica is the source
of Rochester's wealth; his father's adherence to the

rules of primogeniture having denied the second son an inheritance, he is led into a marital exchange by which he acquires thirty thousand pounds and an indissoluble tie to 'tainted' blood, and the Mason family the advantages of connection with his 'good race' (p. 309). This is the story which cannot be fully spoken in the novel: it erupts, nonetheless, in Bertha's wordless laugh and 'eccentric murmurs' (p. 111) and in the document, riven with blanks, that testifies to the unbreakable tie between Rochester and what is secret, shameful and suppressed (p. 293).

There are, I think, ten explicit references to slavery in *Jane Eyre*. They allude to slavery in Ancient Rome and in the seraglio, to the slaveries of paid work as a governess and of dependence as a mistress. None of them refers to the slave trade upon which the fortunes of all in the novel are based. Quakers, of course, had been among the first and most prominent opponents of English slavery, but Jane's own Quakerishness, so often commented upon, leads her only as far as a stern opposition to distant or metaphorical forms of enslavement.[10] This brings us close to one of the central problems of the novel, and in turn of certain kinds of feminist readings of it: the apparently blithe predication of the liberty and happiness of a few upon the confinement and suffering of the many. There is a single glimpse of this, in a different sort of context, during the episode of the typhus epidemic at Lowood, when Jane first begins to explore those 'prospects' in the wider world to which the novel so often adverts: she remarks here, as she will remark nowhere else, that 'for this unwonted liberty and pleasure, there was a cause' (p. 77). And that cause is, precisely, that other girls cannot go where she is freed to go.

In saying this, I do not wish for a moment to deny that *Jane Eyre* can bring all the pleasures of a paradigmatic 'woman's novel'. It is a canonical novel in a 'high' genre, the *Bildungsroman*, composed of the intermingling and collision of a number of 'low' or para-literary forms, many of them associated with women as readers or writers: the Gothic novel, the ballad, the folk-tale, the fairy-tale, romantic fiction, the governess novel, children's fiction, spiritual auto-biography, have all been detected within it, and some of them discussed in detail.[11] The point is that contemporary feminist criticism must not, surely, reproduce the silences and occlusions of nineteenth-century English culture in allowing the white, middle-class woman to stand as its own 'paradigmatic woman'. Of course, generations of female readers have thrilled to Jane's double success story, to the vindication of her principles and the high romance of her return to Rochester, though a not uncommon sneaking dissatisfaction with the last chapters betrays, I think, an awareness of its mystification, through the notorious literalised pun that is Rochester's telepathic summons, of the 'vocation' of the woman. I do not think it is necessary to take an accusatory attitude towards Brontë (and it is clearly futile to take such a stance towards Jane) in order to analyse what is happening in *Jane Eyre*: it is possible to trace in the trajectory, in the very form of the novel, a complex configuration of the determinations of class, kin, gender and – what is nowhere spoken but is omnipresent – race that interacts and conflicts to turn Jane Eyre the ' "mad cat" ' (p. 12) and 'revolted slave' (p. 14) of the opening into the Mrs Rochester of the close. The difficulty is to honour what can be honoured of its female heroism without suppressing a recognition of the social formation to which, along with her twenty thousand pounds, Jane is heir.

Mothers and fathers

It has been suggested that there is a matriarchal story within *Jane Eyre*, of Jane's turning to and learning from mother figures.[12] There is the shadow of such a narrative in the novel, but it is, I think, a defeatist one in which Jane tests the limits of a mother-centred world and is turned back to the patriarchal determinations of kinship and inheritance. In any case, it is important to note at the outset that Jane begins less as a conscientious objector to the patriarchal organisation of society than as an outcast from it. Her earliest awareness of injustice results, not particularly from generalised or abstract principle, but rather from the sense of being denied what is rightfully hers – and ultimately, of course, she will be shown to be justified in this. This sense becomes apparent even on the opening page, when the initial first-person plural – 'we had been wandering . . . in the leafless shrubbery' (p. 7) – splits as Jane is marked as, grammatically even, not one of us. The pain of this split for her is recorded in a sentence where syntactical inversion serves to assert simultaneously her self-awareness and the unnaturalness of the event: 'Me, she had dispensed from joining the group' (p. 7). This exclusion from the family grouping – one repeated and finally overcome in the recurrence of that particular family configuration (mother, brother, two sisters) in the novel – brings with it, as it must, an exile from class: ' "You are a dependent, mama says; you have no money; your father left you none; you ought to beg, and not to live here with gentlemen's children like us" ' (p. 11). John Reed, too, is proved right: Jane does come to beg, and only when she finds an inheritance is she able to live on terms of equality with 'gentlemen's children'. Bessie confirms that Jane's class position is less a descent than a state of suspension: ' "You are less than a servant, for you do nothing for your keep" ' (p. 12). And patriarchy is at once built into this double rejection: ' "Now, I'll teach you to rummage my bookshelves: for they *are* mine; all the house belongs to me, or will do in a few years" ' (p. 11). All, then – family, class, inheritance – hinges upon patrilineage. That culture, too, has a double role in the house of the master, that books have power to *hurt* as well as to enlarge horizons, is also apparent when the very book she has found 'profoundly interesting' (p. 9), however mysterious, is flung at her head and cuts it open. So Jane is triply disinherited in the first chapter of the novel, while obliged to live within the structures of inheritance, and hence that very poignant moment when she feels 'an inexpressible relief, a soothing conviction of protection and security, when I knew there was a stranger in the room' (p. 19).

The later Jane, the narrator, offers a retrospective justification of the behaviour of the Reeds by suggesting that neither the kinship of likeness ('I was like nobody there' (p. 15)) nor the kinship of the family ('They were not bound to regard with affection . . . a heterogeneous thing' (p.15)) obliges them to any more humane treatment. The novel will continue to explore this double meaning of kinship – being like, being related – until their triumphal reinstatement at the ending, with the finding of the Rivers family and her marriage with Rochester. Here, though, Jane's initial weapon and revenge against persecution comes in the first of those instances when 'something' not herself speaks through her; here, she all but ventriloquises the voice of Uncle Reed: 'something spoke out of me over which I had no control' (p. 27). Her question, so terrible as to strike her aunt dumb, is ' "What would Uncle Reed say to you if he were alive?" ' (p. 27), and it asserts not (or not only) a generalised moral reproach, but the power of the family and of the father within it. Elaine Showalter has remarked on the fact that *Jane Eyre* is virtually peopled with female surrogates for absent powerful males[13] – Mrs Reed, Miss Temple, Mrs Fairfax, Grace Poole – but it is remarkable that only Jane, here briefly among them, takes on the unique power of invoking (not, of course, uttering) the very words of this absentee landlord of patriarchal ideology.

So, then, Mrs Reed the archetypal 'bad mother' figure is rebuked by means of the authority of the father figure, and this sets the pattern for a series of neglectful, powerless or inadequate surrogate mothers in the novel. Miss Temple, for example, who 'had stood me in the stead of mother' (p. 85), now marries and leaves the community of women that is Lowood, and Jane's comments on the event leave no doubt that she regards this as in some part a defection: she 'was lost to me' and 'with her was gone every settled feeling, every association that had made Lowood in some degree a home to me' (pp. 84–5). Mrs Fairfax, at first sight such a grandmotherly figure with her 'widow's cap, black silk gown and snowy muslin apron . . . occupied in knitting' (p. 96), soon proves to be 'no great dame, but a dependent like my self' (p. 101) and thus as disqualified from power as Jane. As mother, in any case, Mrs

Fairfax proves of no assistance: she sees, and attempts to communicate, that Jane is in great danger, but can do nothing about it. After the revelation of Bertha's continuing existence and wifely status, it is in following the advice of the moon-mother in her 'trance-like dream' (p. 324) that Jane is brought to her lowest point in the novel (though, arguably, by the intervention of providence, also to family and fortune). The moon's advice – ' "My daughter, flee temptation" ' (p. 324) – is one of a number of transposed Biblical and religious references in the novel that interact with its anti-clericalism to adumbrate a possible female-centred religion;[14] it seems almost an answer to that part of the Lord's Prayer – addressed as it is to our *Father* – in which Christians ask 'Lead us not into temptation'.

But when Jane leaves Thornfield, fleeing temptation at the behest of the mother, she becomes absolutely destitute, without family or money or possessions of any sort. According to Gilbert and Gubar, the moment on the heath is emblematic of 'the essential homelessness – the nameless, placeless and contingent status – of women in a patriarchal society';[15] we surely do not need to accept this idea of 'essential contingency', though, to see how Jane here functions as the very type of the woman falling (or forced) outside all those structures – family, marriage, class, work – by which a patriarchal ordering of society is structured and replicates itself. It is at this point that Jane, with no point of anchorage in the patriarchal society which is the only society available to her, makes her sole reference to 'the universal mother, Nature: I will suck her breast and ask repose' (p. 327). This 'universal mother' proves, however, to be without nourishment. Mothers and daughters stand in somewhat fraught relations in the novel, and not least because daughters can always, through that lawful sexuality of the marriage bed which is itself imaged in Bertha as monstrous,[16] become mothers – Jane's child-dreams, in which the child proves a burden and the mother an unsafe refuge, pick up the threatening instability of the relationship. Jane Eyre, and *Jane Eyre*, derive a double power from the *appetitive* representation of the woman – those famous images of hunger are the vehicle not only of a general deprivation, after all, but also of instinctual appetite – and from the possibility of the woman's refusal to satisfy it; Jane refuses to eat as often as she eats in the novel.[17] But here, on the heath, instinctual appetite is shown to demand satisfaction within the social world and the breast of the 'universal mother' nourishes only within the asocial world of the natural. Lizards and bees, perhaps, find what they need, 'But I was a human being, and had a human being's wants: I must not linger where there was nothing to supply them' (p. 329). The mothering moon of myth and the mothering earth of nature cannot fulfil the most minimal needs of the woman as fully social being, and this fantasied matriarchal world has no power within the world of social organisation that is necessary for survival.[18]

But a return to such a society is not easy for a woman 'without a resource: without a friend: without a coin' (pp. 330–1), and Jane's question of survival – ' "And what do the women do?" ' (p. 331) – has no easy or satisfactory answer: ' "I know n't," was the answer. "Some does one thing, and some another. Poor folk mun get on as they can" ' (p. 331). What the women do, it seems, is reinforce and enforce the power of those patriarchal structures Jane seems at this point to evade. Her attempts, at this moment of fullest deprivation and exile, to effect a re-entry into social structures are made through appeal to women. And all of them – the baker, the woman who does not want a servant, and finally Hannah – rebuff her; the most that is on offer is a mess of rejected pigswill. Refused entry, Jane finally collapses at the very door of a houseful of women: 'Alas, this isolation – this banishment from my kind!' (p. 340). Only the returning St John, like some sanctified John Reed, has the power to admit the beggar into the house of gentlemen's children, and his first act is to acknowledge, but also to take control over, that unsatisfied appetite that has structured her narrative thus far: ' "Not too much at first – restrain her . . . she has had enough!" And he withdrew the cup of milk and the plate of bread' (p. 341).

Thereafter begins Jane's full incorporation into patriarchal society; and with it, as Jina Politi has noted, begins the novel's definitive shift away from the social determinations of realist narration and into the plot concatenations of accident, coincidence, miracle.[19] In short, thereafter begins the fullest sense of the providential narrative, the story dispensed and directed by Our Father, in which the woman who comes to know her place (her origin, her family, her marriage) inherits the earth. And, as if to reinforce this point, the providential theme means that what Jane receives is what was always meant for her; the money she acquires is no mysterious gratuity, but an inheritance that ties her fully into family, home and class by its assertion of kin. With this confirmation of kindred as relationship behind her, Jane is empowered to make the choice of kinship as likeness in her marriage; and her choice of the gentleman Rochester serves in its turn to confirm the status of 'lady' which was clearly always in some sense hers. Bessie has expressed this clearly earlier in the novel: ' "Oh you are quite a lady, Miss Jane! I knew you would be" ' (p. 93), and Jane later authorises it unequivocally: 'Bessie Leaven had said I was quite a lady; and she spoke truth; I was a lady' (p. 159).

For while Jane has sometimes been economically and socially dependent, her perceptions of her own class status have been unwavering; she has from the first rejected the possibility of ' "belong[ing] to poor people" ' (p. 24), even to the point of asserting allegiances of class over those of blood. Patronage is the tone which belongs to her dealings with all those who fall beneath her perception of herself in terms of class or English-ness; 'docile' is her highest term of approbation for such characters, as for her Yorkshire pupils and the reconstructed, 'de-Frenchified' Adèle. She is surprised to find of her 'heavy-looking, gaping rustics' that 'there was a difference amongst them as amongst the educated' (p. 370); and her greatest intimate among the servants she deals with is called Leaven, as if to note her role in what is otherwise, for Jane, the lump of the working class. Even at her moment of greatest deprivation, this class feeling is clearly in evidence. As Jane stands, penniless and half-starved, outside the window of the Rivers home, she sees a clean and modestly furnished room, and 'an elderly woman, somewhat rough-looking, but scrupulously clean, like all about her' (p. 336). Her comment upon the scene assimilates Hannah the servant into the furniture: 'I noticed these *objects* cursorily only' (p. 336; my italics). On the other hand, Diana and Mary, 'young, graceful women – ladies in every point' form 'a group of more interest' (p. 336). Jane's sense of the relationship between the three women turns entirely upon the sense – shared with some others (less infallible readers than Jane) in the novel – that class is written legibly upon the body: 'they could not be the daughters of the elderly person at the table; for she looked like a rustic, and they were all delicacy and cultivation' (p. 335). Jane, 'outcast, vagrant, and disowned by the wide world' (p. 342) though she is at this point, nevertheless retains a sense of class affiliation that has nothing to do with economics;[20] her reproof to Hannah is that she has ' "made it a species of reproach that I had no 'brass' and no house" ' (p. 347), but Hannah's error has been, not a lack of charitable response, but rather ' "supposing me a beggar. I am no beggar . . . in your sense of the word" ' (p. 345). This correction is underwritten and authorised by her assertion that she is ' "very . . . book-learned" ' (p. 345). Jane, then, is not what she seems, no beggar even when she is undeniably begging, and that is because she is *naturally* a lady.

The idea of a natural status is closely tied to the idea of a natural character which figures prominently in the novel, reinforced by the use of physiognomy and phrenology to describe and delimit the characters; these pseudo-sciences offer a reading of character that, for the skilled reader, is immediate and unchangeable, though it is possible to fail to fulfil the potential they imply.[21] So it is that Rochester is 'naturally a man of better tendencies, higher principles, and purer tastes than such as circumstances had developed' (p. 148), and so is 'naturally and inevitably loved' by Jane (p. 254). Bertha's ' "pigmy intellect" ' and ' "giant propensities" ' result from ' "a nature the most gross, impure, depraved I ever saw" ' (p. 311); and mistresses are "often by nature, and always by position, inferior" '

(p. 316). What is odd about Jane's relation to all of this is that being 'natural' is something that does not come naturally to her; it is something which she must grow into. Mrs Reed cannot love her or accept her into the family until she acquires ' "a more . . . child-like disposition . . . something lighter, franker, more natural, as it were' " (p. 7), for instance, and Rochester hopes that ' "in time . . . you will learn to be natural with me" ' (p. 140). So, neither the early rebellious Jane nor the middle-period subdued Jane is 'natural', or rather they are not seen as such. And, although this has obviously to do with repressions and restrictions, it also suggests that neither the propertyless dependent nor the paid employee is the 'real', the 'natural' Jane. That character emerges only after the discovery of the inheritance, and she is Jane the natural lady whose rebellion gives way to complicity and whose wish for paid work and wide horizons is overtaken by the sense that ' "domestic endearments and household joys" ' are ' "the best things the world has" ' (p. 395).

The languages of class and of political conflict come, in the course of the novel, to be eroticised into a language of affinity and mutual dependence. Just as 'master' changes as the narrative progresses from representing a brutal assertion of power and privilege (John Reed's insistence on being called ' "*Master* Reed " ' (p. 9)) to the mark of an intimate and voluntary submission (' "my dear Master . . . I am come back to you" ' (p. 439)), so too the child Jane who opposes her doctrine of revolt to Helen's defence of Charles I (p. 57) becomes the woman who fantasises erotic flirtation in terms of sultans and slaves, ' "aristocratic tastes" ' and ' "plebeian brides" ' (p. 283). This fantasy of a cross-class marriage is supplanted by Jane's apparent transformation from ' "plebeian bride" ' to her ' "own mistress" ' (p. 440), confirming in terms of class the rightness of the marrying couple. Politi has argued that 'Jane runs away so that the workings of Divine Providence may bring about her rise in social status and save her marriage to Mr Rochester from becoming a social offence.'[22] My point is that Jane's 'rise in social status' comes in fact as a confirmation of what is already there rather than a transformation. Nature and providence are invoked to underwrite and reinstate the social institutions of class; marriage to Mr Rochester, then, is the culmination of Jane's installation in the social space Divine Providence and natural character have alike designed for her, and in this way she comes, in the fullest range of senses, to know her place.

'Incident, life, fire, feeling' (p. 110)

In what I have said so far, as in those comments on the novel from Edwards, Politi and Weissman quoted at the beginning of the chapter (and these can be taken to represent a number of other, similar views), it is evident that what is problematic is primarily the ending of the novel, or rather, perhaps, the question of the relation of ending to beginning. The plot trajectory that takes Jane from exile to keeper of the keys, from *déclassée* to lady, from outcast of family structure to restorer and vessel of patrilineage ('the boy had inherited his own eyes' (p. 457)), from defence of the necessity and dignity of work to mystique of the woman's calling: that is what cuts so dramatically and undeniably across those obviously appealing 'heroic' readings of the vindication and achievements of Jane.[23]

It is possible, however, to look at the ending as only one among a series of narrative moments, as Beaty has argued:

> The ending enforces a conservative, conformist, providential reading but it cannot erase the *experience* of the reading, which has involved the projection of alternative configurations over long stretches of the plot and subsumed innumerable details.[24]

That is to say, the sequence of the plot need not abolish the range of narrative possibilities intimated in the course of the text: we need not establish our own unitary and providential narrative of reading to set beside Jane's.

There is, of course, another story to tell in the novel and that is the story that allows her to write her woman's autobiography, not as 'Mrs Edward Rochester' but as Jane Eyre. The fortune which brings about Jane's inheritance of her woman's place also (by alerting her uncle to her intentions) disrupts that tale of ' "the same theme – courtship; and . . . the same catastrophe – marriage" ' (p. 201); what brings her a family also bestows upon her 'an independency' (p. 271). The mechanisms by which Jane progressively gains entry to all that has been denied her, or by which providence and Charlotte Brontë bring about her satisfying revenge on all those who have injured or thwarted her, are in a sense explorations – however tentative, however fantasied – of the kinds and limits of power available to the middle-class white woman in the particular society the novel represents. Jane's *Bildungsroman*, in a way that is probably more characteristic of a hero's than a heroine's text, shows us *what* she learns, shows her at work in the world, shows her, above all, arriving at a choice, albeit a restricted one, of

possible vocations at the end. In the course of the novel
Jane has three jobs, five homes, three families of a sort,
two proposals of marriage. If her travel is restricted, at
least she nearly goes to the South of France, nearly
goes to Madeira, nearly goes to India. She learns
French, German and Hindustani. She lives alone,
receives male visitors in her bedroom in the middle of
the night and hears confidences of financial treachery
and sexual profligacy. She saves a life, proposes
marriage and gives away thousands of pounds. She
longs for broader horizons, pleads for a wider range of
activities for women, gives an impassioned defence of
the right to feeling of those who are ' "poor, obscure,
plain, and little" ' (p. 255). She suffers, fights back,
stands by her principles, vanquishes her enemies, and
ends up 'supremely blest' (p. 456). That Jane's 'calling'
turns out finally to be the voice of Rochester and a
quiet wedding should not obscure the extraordinarily
wide range of narrative possibilities the novel offers its
central female character.

Jane Eyre seems, too, to offer a world of physical
restriction against which she chafes, continually
searching for prospects through windows. And yet, set
against this air of enclosure and restraint there is the
intense and startling physicality of the novel: its evocation of mental and emotional torment through freezing
frosts and blazing fires, the 'disseverment of bone and
vein' (p. 325), floods and shipwrecks, starvation and
punishment. Dreams and omens, natural symbols and
mystic calls – in short the whole panoply of the
supernatural – are enlisted in the service of what
remain, after all, entirely human and secular
appetites.[25] Jane's inner life, whatever her modest
demeanour, seems to rage across heaven and earth in a

kind of cosmic psychodrama. And all of this, of course, in Charlotte Brontë's 'fortissimo' style.[26]

This singleness of focus extends even to making most of the characters projections or fragments of Jane Eyre, J.E., 'je', the narrating 'I'. They seem to be called up – as it were materialised – by Jane's needs and experiments, as Karen Chase has demonstrated;[27] so, when Mrs Reed demands ' "perfect submission and stillness" ' (p. 18) as the condition of liberation, Helen embodies these qualities and their limitations as tactics of survival; Jane pleads for ' "a new servitude" ' (p. 86) and Mr Rochester literally falls at her feet; she longs for 'incident, life, fire, feeling' (p. 110) and Bertha's mirthless laugh offers a sardonic commentary on what these may mean; and when Jane seeks to become 'ice and rock' (p. 304) and to live by religious principle, St John Rivers appears with his dangerously tempting offer of the undelighting rigours of a missionary position. That Jane, 'witch' as Rochester frequently calls her, has brought these characters into being is clear partly in the often abrupt and mysterious manner of their appearance – Rochester's dim arrival through the dusk, St. John's disembodied voice (' "All men must die" ' (p. 340)) in response to her resignation to the will of God.

And it is notable that almost all who come into contact with Jane are burned, singed, seared: Helen burns with consumption, Bertha – the 'Angria' version of Mrs Rochester – leaps into the flames she has kindled on what she believes to be her rival's bed, St John Rivers 'hides a fever in his vitals' (p. 361), Rochester is seared in eye and hand before he can have her. It is as if the passion of the unsatisfied Jane will consume what threatens or denies her, just as the inflammatory passion of the actress Vashti, in *Villette*, will make the theatre burst into flames. But Jane is saved from spontaneous combustion; as St Paul and *Jane Eyre* in their different ways affirm, it is better to marry than to burn, and the 'socialization of the psyche', in Pell's phrase,[28] ultimately reduces Jane's cosmic passions to the less terrifying dimensions of the dank and insalubrious Ferndean.

This story of passion, ambition and power continually restates and challenges that contradiction between feminine and heroic character ideals, self-abnegation and self-assertion, so common in Victorian novels centring upon a growing woman.[29] There is, unquestionably, a heroic narrative of consciousness in *Jane Eyre* in which self-assertion threatens an expansion that will absorb the whole world, but this fantasied female power is continually tethered and troubled by the realist narrative of social determination and patriarchal imbrication. It is the tension between the two – sometimes seen as an opposition between Gothic and realist elements, or Romantic and realist, or fairy-tale and novel – that gives this novel its peculiar intensity and force, acting out as it does at the very level of form the mutual dependencies and incompatibilities of desire and restraint.

Chapter Three

Shirley

'The toad in the block of marble'[1]

Shirley has often been described, accurately enough, as Brontë's Thackerayan novel, as an attempt at a social panorama. Despite this panoramic impulse, however, the character who provides the novel with its central female consciousness, Caroline Helstone, seems more cramped and confined than any other of Brontë's heroines. Her world is restricted physically and limited socially, as theirs are, but also attenuated emotionally; she has none of the fire-raising, tempest-inducing passion of Jane Eyre or Lucy Snowe. The wider focus of the novel serves only to bring into clearer focus the restraints upon Caroline's health and well-being, denied meaningful employment as she is and, for much of the novel, also denied love, in what is clearly always for Brontë the greatest deprivation imaginable. Whereas all the other main characters of the novel are linked with the possibility of some form of emigration (the fantasied Americas of Louis Moore and Shirley, the southern hemisphere of the Yorke sisters, the exile of bankruptcy in the case of Robert Moore), Caroline has only one connection with the wider world beyond Yorkshire. That link is her sewing for the 'Jew-basket', the proceeds of which are to be 'applied to the conversion of the Jews, the seeking up of the ten missing tribes, or to the regeneration of the interesting coloured populations of the globe' (p. 112). The sneering tone of this illustrates, not only a fairly commonplace Victorian racism, but also what has happened to the heroic missionary narrative of *Jane Eyre*, one in which it was conceivable for a woman to take an active part; here, by contrast, the 'Jew-basket' at each occurrence serves as the very emblem of futility and of the trivialisation of women's talents. All the usual avocations of the Victorian middle-class lady – running the home, charitable work, sewing – are seen in the course of the novel as comical or pointless or stultifying. Caroline pleads for the chance to work at something more, though in such timorous terms that Brontë's more adventurously feminist friend Mary Taylor wrote from New Zealand to comment upon them:

> I have seen some extracts from *Shirley*, in which you talk of women working. And this first duty, this great necessity, you seem to think that some women may indulge in – if they give up marriage and don't make themselves too disagreeable to the other sex. You are a coward and a traitor.[2]

This work is never a fully realised project, however; what seems most important to Caroline is perhaps rather the chance simply to move: ' "I should be well if I went from home" ' (p. 189).[3] To be well is to be able to move, to leave home, as the child Jessie Yorke stresses in one of those catechistic dialogues in which the novel abounds:

> 'Should I be happier wandering alone in strange countries, as you wish to do?'
> 'Much happier, even if you did nothing but wander . . . if you only went on and on, like some enchanted lady in a fairy tale, you might be happier than now.' (p. 399)

To set against the obtrusive regional chauvinism of *Shirley* is this sense that to stay still is to risk misery and illness.

It is surely significant here that, where the names of Eyre and Snowe invoke elemental movement and fluidity, Caroline's name links her with stone, with what is by contrast fixed and immovable. Caroline's life, according to Jessie Yorke, is ' "a black trance like the toad's, buried in marble" ' (p. 399): the hell within the stone. And if Caroline is to follow the exhortations of the narrator, to 'endure without a sob' the scorpion's sting or the stone given where bread is asked (p. 105), then she risks only a future of imprisonment like that of the silent and neglected Mary Cave,[4] 'a girl of living marble' (p. 52) whose endurance without a sob has concealed both pain and need:

> He thought, so long as a woman was silent, nothing ailed her, and she wanted nothing. If she did not complain of solitude, solitude, however continued, would not be irksome to her. If she did not talk and put herself forward, express a partiality for this, an aversion to that, she had no partialities or aversions, and it was useless to consult her tastes. (p. 53)

Shirley is itself caught, in its representations of both class and gender oppressions, in a radical divide between the drives toward silent stoicism and toward loud revolt, toward resigned stillness and vigorous movement. Stoicism can bring the fate of Mary Cave, revolt the fate of the transported workers. Shirley, tamed by love for Louis, nevertheless fears that she incubates within her the rage of the dog Phoebe, biting the hand that charitably feeds her. And revolt can be imaged in the 'half-crazed' Antinomian weaver and 'mad leveller' Mike Hartley (p. 635), the spectre of madness and moral anarchism who (in a structural parallel with the dog attack that says much about the novel's depiction of working-class action) shoots the newly paternalistic Robert. Movement holds its dangers, too. 'Abroad', in this novel, can be both a lure and a threat, at once the home of the true poetry (Chenier and Rousseau) and the home of the 'poisoned exhalations of the East' (p. 421) that enfever Caroline. Movement brings her Robert, from France; movement threatens to take him away from her again, to Canada. Shirley fantasies a life as ' "the slave-wife of the Indian chief" ' in North America (p. 468) as a way of escaping social duty; Louis imagines a life with Liberty as his bride in the ' "virgin woods" ' (p. 614) of the ' "wild West" ' (p. 613). Both settle for Yorkshire and a comfortable income instead. Robert plans to go to Canada and start again, until restored to solvency by the repeal of the Orders in Council. But there are two groups within the novel that do make their voyages: the labour leaders, transported to Australia, and the Yorke sisters, in revolt against the ' "long, slow death" ' of the womanly life (p. 399), whom the 'magic mirror' of prospective narration shows us 'in some region of the southern hemisphere' (p. 150). The novel's Yorkshire expels its dissidents. It is a sign at once of great pessimism and of great conservatism that the stories of social reordering and transformation will be confided to a future invisible to the novel, to a southern hemisphere apparently annexed as both unpeopled and ideologically 'empty'.

'Capsized by the patriarch bull' (p. 245)

Shirley is structured around polarised masculine and feminine worlds, as Pauline Nestor has shown.[5] The mill versus the home, industry versus nature, head versus heart: all of these are familiar enough ideological oppositions. But a less obviously gendered polarity of no less importance to the novel is that variously presented as plain narrative versus poetry, the real world versus utopia, common sense versus fantasy: what might be called, in brief, realism versus rhapsody. The central female characters are consistently associated with the second, in differing degrees: one of the ways in which Caroline is a 'pencil-sketch' (p. 249) to Shirley's 'vivid painting' (p. 250) is their differential relation to this realism/rhapsody opposition. Caroline may on occasion be a ' "bookish, romancing chit of a girl" ' (p. 404), but it is primarily Shirley who bears the novel's linguistic theme. Both women offer passionate defences of poetry, and both, indeed, are silent, unwritten poets. Caroline hears words in the wind:

> 'Why, it suggested to me words one night: it poured a strain which I could have written down, only I was appalled, and dared not rise to seek pencil and paper by the dim watch-light.' (p. 427)

Characteristically, it is Caroline's timorousness that prevents her turning her inspirations into poetry, while Shirley is held back by indolence and a kind of innocent self-undervaluing: 'She does not know, has never known, and will die without knowing, the full value of that spring whose bright fresh bubbling in her heart keeps it green' (p. 388). The novel's only male 'poet', on the other hand, is Sir Philip Nunnely, who is mocked for his inability to write anything more than verse.

Nor is this a schematically applied opposition at the level of theme alone; *Shirley*, a novel whose disunity cannot but strike even the most organicist of readers, gives this impression partly because it operates two distinct strains of writing. There is the plain narrative, 'unromantic as Monday morning' (p. 5), that sets out to detail industrial conflict in West Yorkshire and abuses within the Anglican church, and then there are the set-pieces of vision, incantation and allegory that enter the novel with Shirley herself. Tess Cosslett has drawn attention to the way in which, in the nineteenth-century novel, relationships between women tend to fall outside the events of the novel; they are often, she suggests, perceived as static, whereas male figures are 'thought to be needed to create tensions and initiate significant action'.[6] Certainly, here, it is evident that the male characters carry forward the plot, fighting and labouring and proposing and conspiring, while the female characters, in Patricia Parker's term, dilate, delaying and expanding 'plain narrative' by their very presence.[7] Caroline's is a woman's story that abuts plain narrative in its attention to social determinations, while Shirley's, in a sense the 'same' story, draws upon allegory and utopia. It is Shirley who can indulge fantasies of transcendence of social determination, in her cross-gender versions of herself as 'Captain Keeldar' and her cross-race imagining of a Rousseauesque noble savagery in the Wild West.[8] She is, Gilbert and Gubar contend, 'Caroline's double, a projection of all her repressed desire',[9] in a sense Caroline's romantic fiction of her own life. Nevertheless, Brontë never allows us to forget that Shirley's fantasies of transcendence are enabled by privileges of class position and wealth; the level of rhapsody of which she is the main vehicle is itself continually grounded in realism.

These 'masculine' and 'feminine' modes of writing connect with the insistence, here, on the images of mutually incomprehensible languages and of translation. ' "I know I speak an unknown tongue," ' says Shirley to her Uncle Sympson, ' " but I feel indifferent whether I am comprehended or not" ' (p. 473). For Sympson, her expression is 'inscrutable . . . as the writing on the wall to Belshazzar' (p. 547), but Louis, to whom he looks for assistance, has 'his own private difficulties connected with that baffling bit of translation' (p. 547). Robert may have difficulties, Caroline thinks, with his mother-in-law: ' "Be sure to let me interpret for her, whenever she puzzles you: always believe my account of the matter, Robert" ' (p. 642). Especially when speaking to men, the women do not, as it were, speak straight: they resort to silence, like Mary Cave, or else they become oracles, sphinxes:

'About each birthday, the spirit moves me to deliver one oracle respecting my own instruction and management: I utter it and leave it; it is for you mother, to listen or not.' (p. 401)

Men and women may need a little simultaneous translation in order to communicate at all, although ' "women read men more truly than men read women" ' (p. 352). Hence, at least in part, the foreignness to one another of each pair of lovers. Both Robert and Louis are shown teaching their lovers to speak their language, and Shirley finds 'lively excitement in the pleasure of making his language her own' (p. 494).[10] By the end of the novel, too, Shirley has ' "inspired romance" ' into the ' "prosaic composition" ' of Louis (p. 522), and Caroline has helped Robert to find the silent poet in himself: ' "Your heart is a lyre, Robert; but the lot of your life has not been a minstrel to sweep it, and it is often silent" ' (p. 89). Again, the image of incomprehensible language is also reflected in the activities of the narration, which translates the powerless speakers for its presumedly middle-class and often male readers; the Luddites' message to Robert must be 'translate[d] . . . into legible English' (p. 33), and Shirley's *devoir* is also translated 'on pain of being unintelligible to some readers' (p. 485). The 'Old Maids' are never permitted to speak; the narrator interposes between them and the reader. And most significantly and remarkably, in the latter stages of the novel, Shirley herself, the main speaker of the 'women's language', loses her right to direct speech; her rejection of Robert and her acceptance of Louis are given to us through the words of the men, in indirect speech, as a character in their stories. But *Shirley* as a whole, of course, never fully effects that suppression of the women's discourse of myth and rhapsody that could re-establish as its dominant form the linear plot of the historical novel. The novel does not surrender poetry and fantasy; its form enacts their disruption of the industrial narrative, and its narrative voice (un-gendered for the only time in Brontë's fiction) embodies an uneasy integration of the two.[11]

These literary compositions of Louis and Shirley take their place among a range of other texts extensively referred to in the novel. Its fictionality is overtly recognised in a number of Thackerayan direct addresses to the reader, commenting on its 'un-romantic' opening, its unmoralised ending, its differences from other industrial novels, for instance. There are a number of sly self-ironies: Mrs Pryor disapproves of the younger women's discussion of the mermaid they have envisioned: ' "We are aware that mermaids do not exist. . . . How can you find interest in speaking of a non-entity?" ' (p. 246). The novel opens, too, with some of Brontë's favourite images, the weather and food, used somewhat humorously, and there is surely an element of self-mockery in Mrs Gale's response to the all-consuming curates: ' "c'en est trop," she would say, if she could speak French' (p. 8). There is in general an explicit interdependence of the fictional real life of the novel and its real-life fictions: Caroline's life, near the beginning of the novel, is a 'narrative of life . . . yet to be commenced' (p. 97), while Bunyan's *The Pilgrim's Progress* is invoked (p. 56) in parallel to historical events. There are, too, the usual acidulous comments on the relation of images of women in men's art and her own heroines; the most interesting of these, I think, is Shirley's account of the ' "Temptress-terror! monstrous likeness of ourselves!" ' (p. 246), the mermaid with her mirror whose glance leads men to destruction. Caroline objects:

'But, Shirley, she is not like us: we are neither temptresses, nor terrors, nor monsters.'
'Some of our kind, it is said, are all three. There are men who ascribe to "woman", in general, such attributes.' (p. 246)

This is surely Brontë's response to her own admired Thackeray, whose *Vanity Fair* (often cited as a model for the panoramic world, social comedy, double heroines, and narratorial addresses of *Shirley*) includes the following comment on his Becky:

> In describing this siren, singing and smiling, coaxing and cajoling, the author, with modest pride, asks his readers all round, has he once forgotten the laws of politeness, and showed the monster's hideous tail above water? . . . They look pretty enough when they sit upon a rock, twangling their harps and combing their hair, and sing, and beckon to you to come and hold the looking-glass; but when they sink into their native element, depend upon it those mermaids are about no good, and we had best not examine the fiendish marine cannibals, revelling and feasting on their wretched pickled victims.[12]

From this kind of dialogue with other texts there emerges a stress upon the possibility of alternative readings, for particular social and political ends. Yorke and Helstone, for example, agree upon the Biblical story of Moses crossing the Red Sea as an apt comparison for the hostilities between France and Britain, and yet they apply it differently: ' "You are all right, only you forget the true parallel. France is Israel, and Napoleon is Moses" ' (p. 39). More commonly, a 'man's' and a 'woman's' reading are proposed. Shirley's onslaught on Milton's Eve is probably the most famous example, but there are also discussions of the biblical Eve, Solomon's virtuous woman, Lucretia, and the parable of the talents which draw out from these texts feminist, or at least woman-centred, interpretations. The matter is raised explicitly when Joe Scott invokes St Paul's words, 'Let the woman learn in silence, with all subjection.' It is in this instance Caroline who argues in favour of appropriative reading:

> 'It would be possible, I doubt not, with a little ingenuity, to

give the passage quite a contrary turn; to make it say, "Let the woman speak out whenever she sees fit to make an objection;" – "it is permitted to a woman to teach and exercise authority as much as may be. Man, meantime, cannot do better than hold his peace," and so on.' (pp. 329–30)

The novel's registering of its own fictionality goes beyond a simple self-reflexivity to pose a certain challenge to the reader. Not merely the tale of *Shirley. A Tale,* but the historical relations of class and gender of which it is a representation, are recognised as matters of contention; struggle for meaning and struggle for power are shown to be thoroughly interconnected. The relations between history and story, text and interpretation, are so problematised that the novel's closing comments are a good deal more than a humorous disclaimer:

> The story is told. I think I now see the judicious reader putting on his spectacles to look for the moral. It would be an insult to his sagacity to offer directions. I only say, God speed him in the quest! (p. 646)

These examples of reading otherwise that I have mentioned above form part of the novel's adumbration of a female religion, centred upon the figure of Eve as mother of humanity. Shirley and Caroline, declining to enter the church at whose gate they stand, enter instead into the vision of the natural world as the primordial mother's body: ' "I will stay out here with my mother Eve, in these days called Nature" ' (p. 321). Eve, as mother, predated ' "the first men of the earth" ' and ' "the first woman's breast that heaved with life on this world" ' gave suck to the generations that were to bring forth the Messiah (p. 320). (The role of Caroline's literal mother should not be forgotten here: her name is, precisely, Pryor.) Adam recedes into the background for much of this vision, but when he does appear, it is in a relation to Eve of parity rather than priority: ' "Eve is Jehovah's daughter, as Adam was his son" ' (p. 321). The central vision – it occurs almost exactly halfway through the novel – joins with the evident anti-clericalism and the valuing of intuitional knowledge over rationality to suggest an alternative, a path not taken, that is not wholly undermined by the women's willing enlistment in the ranks of the Anglicans in their semi-comic Whitsuntide battle against the Dissenters. This religious feminism is reinforced by a strain of diabolic imagery focused upon the male characters: Robert Moore is addressed by the Luddites as ' "the Divil of Hollow's-miln" ' (p. 33), and Mr Yorke is 'haughty as Beelzebub' (p. 47). Robert Moore, proposing to Shirley for her money, repeats the expulsion of Lucifer: ' "Lucifer – Star of the Morning! . . . thou art fallen" ' (p. 536). By contrast Shirley, who doodles 'broken crosses' while discussing her early *devoir* (p. 490), and Mrs Pryor both sing in voices angelic or even 'almost divine' (p. 431). Of course, Brontë's more orthodox (and sectarian) Protestant piety is also present throughout the novel, but it has here less power to console, reconcile or justify than anywhere else in her adult fiction.

The paganised Eve, mother of Titans, and the community of women hinted at in the women's attraction toward the conventual Nunnwood, constitute their own commentary upon the male-centred church in the world. They posit heroically feminine values under threat in the industrialising world of the novel, values associated with the vanishing 'fairishes' of the end (p. 646). For the oppressed (here, women), myth can appear as a disruption of and an alternative to that history whose terms and course have been set by the powerful. It is true that the feminist myth of a power that resides *within* the feminine sphere of personal relationship, family and nurturance unsettles what Rabine calls the 'official masculine historicity'[13] that gives industrial and political struggle primacy. But this alternative is constituted as such only within a system of polarities – female versus male, personal versus political, family versus employment – that registers and preserves the exclusion of women from the historicity of class and workplace. The ideological value of the myth offers a strategy for consolation, not for change. In this respect, the shadowy feminist religion of *Shirley* is a fantasied way of bringing together the urges towards social transformation and stoic acceptance in the novel, implying an overturning of the relative valuations of masculine and feminine spheres while leaving untouched, more or less, the delineation of the polarity and, with it, the existing distribution of power. Feminist protest is recuperated into retrospective fantasy, power in the world ceded in return for a spiritual superiority. The circular chain binding together nature/instinct/motherhood/woman is an ideological tripwire over which feminism has more than once fallen.[14]

Although these mythological forms of female power are stated in a retrospective narrative of fall and loss, there is also a forward chronological movement by which a generational change among the women characters is implicitly proposed. The older women in the book – the counterposed characters of Hortense and Mrs Yorke, for example – are truculently concerned only with their roles in relation to homes and men, or else (like Miss Ainsley), lacking the good fortune to have men in their homes, with those charitable works that are the mainstay of genteel femininity in the period. The novel's youngest women, Rose and Jessie Yorke, by contrast, while not undervaluing the skills of domestic labour (' "I should be sorry not to learn to sew: you do right to teach me, and to make me work' " (p. 401)) are able also to envisage another life for themselves (' "Am I to do nothing but that? I will do that, and then I will do more" ' (p. 401)), even if that 'more' requires exile from the known community. Poised uneasily between the two groups stand Caroline and Shirley, able to envisage new relationships and interdependences beyond the conjugal, but still unable to find the strength or the society to practise them. Marriage, it is clear, comes to be validated only at the end of *Shirley*; otherwise it has been presented in a strongly negative light, both in principle and in practice, and especially so for women:

> '[Marriage] is never wholly happy. Two people can never literally be as one: there is, perhaps, a possibility of content under peculiar circumstances, such as are seldom combined; but it is as well not to run the risk: you may make fatal mistakes. Be satisfied, my dear; let all the single be satisfied with their freedom.' (p. 379)[15]

In the course of the novel, a number of other possibilities of relationship are examined. There are the 'old maids', for example, who, however patronisingly presented, are nevertheless found ultimately to have stories and worth of their own. Miss Ainsley, indeed, is an explicitly Christ-like figure of celibacy. Even if Miss Mann is a 'Medusa' (p. 178) in Robert Moore's imaginings, it is not she who turns the women to stone; it is rather the ' "long, black trance" ' (p. 399) of femininity, of waiting for life to begin with a husband, that does that. Then, too, *Shirley* presents an unusually large number of non-marital households, uncles and nieces or brothers and sisters, in which male power is none-theless still at issue. Relations of friendship or community among women are suggested in the imagery of nuns and Amazons, and tested out in Caroline and Shirley, who relish their first excursion together partly because it is to be without men: ' "the presence of gentlemen dispels the last charm" ' (p. 214). Their visit is to the very female landscape of the dell, ' "a deep hollow cup" ' (p. 213) wherein they find the ruined convent.

But undoubtedly the chief relationship among women which the novel considers is that of mother and daughter, a relationship explored at the levels of mythology (Eve as first mother, Mother Nature) and of individuals (Mrs Yorke, Mrs Pryor). What Nestor calls 'mother want'[16] is vividly present throughout. It is partly a search for predecessors that will bestow and confirm identity and worth. It also brings about a love powerful enough to bring Caroline back from the brink of death, from an illness triggered by Robert's apparent failure to love her; this interchangeability of maternal and sexual love will be imaged in reverse in Shirley's composition 'The First Blue-Stocking', where the apparently unmothered, unloved Eva ' "should die" ' (p. 486) but is restored by the erotic commingling of Genius and Humanity. But, as this allegory suggests, if 'mother want' in part fuels the novel's feminist impulse throughout, it comes also to undo its anti-marriage theme. The ideological centrality of motherhood in the novel's urging of the claims of the 'feminine sphere' requires, if it is to be translated into the social climate

of the 1840s, a revalidation of marriage: the middle-
class woman has, you might say, to be a 'Mrs' prior to
being a mother, even if the relationship leaves her
' "galled, crushed, paralyzed, dying" ' (p. 437). So it is
that the ' "ordinary destiny" ' of wifedom (p. 174) is
reinstated as the ground and end of being for Shirley
and Caroline. If it is Nature that bestows upon women
alone together ' "peaceful joy" ', then it is equally
Nature that makes of relations with ' "the right sort" '
of young men ' "elation and . . . anxiety" ',
' "excitement . . . and trouble" ' (p. 214). The problem
here is not, I think, the affirmation of heterosexual
relationship in itself, but the unspoken assumption
that this entails an acceptance of the whole train of
consequences of conventional marriage, those very
dependencies, exclusivities, masteries and submissions
that the novel has opened to question in its portrayal of
marital relationships. It is because of the novel's waver-
ing commitments to revolt and resignation that the
critiques of marriage and of male dominance that it has
offered come to be undermined by the fear of
'unwomanliness', of becoming a Captain Keeldar or a
Miss Mann. A certain anxiety creeps into the reassur-
ance that Shirley is ' "girlish: not a man-like woman at
all – not an Amazon" ' (p. 503), that there is ' "nothing
masculine" ' about Caroline (p. 362). To pick up on
Brontë's splendidly mixed metaphor, it is perhaps
because *Shirley* is concentrating so hard on not rocking
the boat that it comes, in the end, to be ' "capsized by
the patriarch bull" ' (p. 245).

'The famished and furious mass' (p. 344)

Shirley, as has often been remarked, sets up a number of

parallels between working-class men and middle-class women; for example, ' "Old maids, like the houseless and unemployed poor, should not ask for a place and an occupation in the world" ' (p. 391). The implicit parallels take in the full range of images of dissatisfaction and deprivation (hunger and starvation, under- and unemployment), as well as emerging through the more analytic account of dependence upon paternalism and patriarchal power. The link between plots of romance centring upon middle-class heroines, and industrial plots of the 'social problem' kind, is not peculiar to Brontë, of course, but is shared with a number of other women writers of the period. As Bodenheimer puts it:

> [T]he newly ornamental lives of genteel women and the newly threatened employment patterns of the industrial working class raise overlapping clusters of fear. Because of that (often submerged) linkage, these novels raise with a special intensity the frequently fictionalized problem of what a heroine is to do with her life.[17]

For Brontë the contradictory urges toward resignation and revolt are there in both plots, and both find a kind of spurious ideological resolution in the paradoxical idea of a free (marital or quasi-feudal) subjection to one who will be master but no tyrant. The representation of revolt is weighted by a kind of social organicism that makes of conflict an image of disease and self-destruction. Shirley argues this point by positing man and woman as interdependent parts of the body:

> 'Shall my left hand dispute for precedence with my right? – shall my heart quarrel with my pulse? – shall my veins be jealous of the blood which fills them?' (p. 219)

When it comes to class, the organicism is less explicitly pronounced, but it is there in, for example, the odd opening metonymies of 'hands' and 'arms' for labour and ruling-class power, and also (tellingly enough in ideological terms) in the opposition of body and soul that appears during the otherwise strikingly dis-embodied allegorical account of the attack on the mill:

> [A]nd the indignant, wronged *spirit* of the middle Rank bears down in zeal and scorn on the famished and furious *mass* of the Operative Class. (p. 344, my italics)

Characteristically, Brontë uses the reading material of her protagonists to reinforce obliquely her own imagery. The supposedly organic nature of the state is, after all, a central presupposition of *Coriolanus*, which Caroline and Robert read together; it is there that we find, in the opening scene, the allegory of the mutiny of 'all the body's members . . . against the belly' on the grounds that it consumes idly and inactively while they must labour.[18] Add to this the somatic determinations of Yorke's political views – being, phrenologically speaking, without the organ of veneration, he is 'intolerant to those above him' and 'very friendly to his workpeople, very good to all who were beneath him' (p. 47) – and the disease imagery of, for example, 'moral scrofula' (p. 132), and there emerges a powerful, if inexplicit, idea of revolt as bodily imbalance or sickness. Since all four of the novel's main characters pass through a period of illness as a marker of the adjust-ment of their own feelings and perspectives, it can be further supposed that, in this novel, Luddism (and probably, therefore, the Chartism of the book's actual time of writing[19]) are no more than the 'poisoned exhalations' (p. 421) from abroad or the bite of mad-dened dogs upon the body politic: revolution as social disease.

Shirley offers no resolution, at the level of argument,

of the class conflict it represents, but it nevertheless has rhetorical and narrative means at its disposal to empty that conflict of its political and historical significance: the continual appeal to a shared quality of 'Yorkshireness' as a cohesive force overriding difference, the organic imagery that serves to bind together in metaphorical interdependence the contending forces it displays, and the introduction of the repeal of the Orders in Council to abolish in fiction the oppositions it merely realigned in history. The novel closes with unities (marriages, a hint of revived feudal communities) but the sense of strain is, I think, quite apparent in the virtual transformation of the industrial theme into a moral testing and growth for Robert Moore, in the late coming to prominence of the safely non-industrial dependence of his brother Louis, and in the chastened tone of the conclusion. Class conflict, like Shirley, seems tamed for the present; but just as she is not turned thereby into a domestic cat, but only into a pantheress gnawing at her chain (p. 629), so there remains, in contradiction to the novel's narrative drive, a sense of subduing by force rather than of voluntary subjection.

The parallels between working-class men and middle-class women provoke their own intractable problems, too. These are related not only to Brontë's own class position but also to the acceptance, here, of masculine and feminine polarities. The working class comes, in effect, to be subsumed into that 'masculine' sphere of industry and conflict which the novel's use of two central female consciousnesses serves to render strange and threatening. Joe Scott is a key figure here, as a worker and a staunch opponent of ' "petticoat government" ' (p. 327). Joe is throughout the novel identified with the interests of his employer, and he also urges strongly Pauline doctrines on that ' "kittle and . . . froward generation" ', women (p. 328). He contradicts flatly the novel's feminist mysticism with his insistence that ' "Adam was first formed, then Eve" ' (p. 329). He may be a kind husband (p. 330) but, unredeemed by the romantic aura of foreignness (and class privilege) that hangs over Robert Moore, it is chiefly he who binds together the industrial strain of the novel and male dominance into its masculine sphere. To set against Joe's worker misogyny, there is the feminisation of William Farren, the novel's representative of the 'good' working-class man. Turned away by unemployment from the industrial sphere, William comes to be progressively identified with nature, which, as I have argued above, is identified as the realm of the feminine.[20] William becomes a gardener, and in so doing he takes on something of the 'language' of women as it is represented by Caroline:

> William and she found plenty to talk about: they had a dozen topics in common; interesting to them, unimportant to the rest of the world. They took a similar interest in animals, birds, insects, and plants; they held similar doctrines about humanity to the lower creation; and had a similar turn for minute observation on points of natural history. (p. 445)

This relationship, though it continues to be one of servant to employer (at the time of these discussions, he is pushing her in her wheelchair around the garden), is shown to evade class, and hence the implication that class (and so class conflict) belongs to the realm of industry that displaces the feminine nature. It is William Farren, incidentally, who foretells the novel's pseudo-resolution in exile; he suggests to Shirley that

' "if ye could transport your tenant, Mr Moore, to Botany Bay, ye'd happen to do better" ' (p. 325). Expulsion will, of course, prove to be the major gesture towards social transformation, but it will be not the employers but the agitators who set off on the long trip to Australia.

In a sense, then, *Shirley* accords its gender schema, the collision of masculine and feminine spheres, priority over its representation of the interests of class: indeed, in the more or less classic fashion of nineteenth-century industrial novels, it will slide class difference beneath gender in order that marriage may effect a reconciliation of sorts at the close. Eagleton has pointed out the novel's narrative disenfranchisement of the working class in the raid on the mill:

> [T]he event is at once structurally central and curiously empty – empty because the major protagonist, the working class, is distinguished primarily by its absence. . . . At the point of its most significant presence in the novel, the working class is wholly invisible.[21]

Helen Taylor, in answer, has pointed out that the scene also dwells upon the marginality and powerlessness of the two women; that there is a stress upon the invisibility to one another of the two groups, of working-class men and of middle-class women.[22] The parallel of the two comes up against the intractability of their different interests, too; the interests, sentimental and financial, of Shirley and Caroline, lie finally with the defence of the machinery. But, true and important as these points are, it seems to me, further, that the overlaying of a particular ideology of gender – one that serves to distance women from the site of work – upon the structures of class has resulted in a significant blind spot. I am thinking here of such as Joe Scott's wife, spoken for by him (' "My wife is a hard-working, plain woman: time and trouble have ta'en all the conceit out of her" ' (p. 330)), and as Mrs Gale, who would have said ' "c'en est trop" . . . if she could speak French' (p. 8) but instead is given nothing to say. The truly invisible, the truly silenced, in *Shirley* are working-class women. That is to say, for most of its length. I could wish to find a political point, and not merely a distancing effect of narration, in the fact that the novel does not end with Robert's paternalistic reformism, or with Louis's diary: it gives the last word to Martha, to a female servant.

Chapter Four

Villette

'I told her a plain tale, which she translated'[1]

Villette is among the strangest of nineteenth-century novels to read. Its fictional world is strikingly unstable: it is haunted by ghostly nuns, undermined by secret burials, and wracked by storms whose emotional and symbolic significance is everywhere apparent, but whose status as narrative events is never unambiguous. It is peopled by name-changers – virtually all the major characters have a variety of names, as Marie Beck is also Modeste Kint, or as the more conventional of the novel's romantic heroes migrates between the names Graham Bretton, Dr John and Isidore – and by shape-changers, characters who apparently become unrecognisable to one another in the course of a few chapters, as Lucy does to her surrogate family the Brettons. On occasion, its narrator seems to take on a full invisibility, as she does in the course of the phantasmagoric night in the park. Curiously perso-

nified (usually female) abstractions behave with extraordinary violence:

> Reason is vindictive as a devil: for me she was always
> envenomed as a step-mother. . . . Often has Reason
> turned me out by night, in mid-winter, on cold snow,
> flinging for sustenance the gnawed bone dogs had
> forsaken . . . . (pp. 225–6.)

Or:

> Sleep went quite away. I used to rise in the night, look
> round for her, beseech her earnestly to return. . . . Sleep
> never came!
> I err. She came once, but in anger. Impatient of my
> importunity she brought with her an avenging dream. By
> the clock of St. Jean Baptiste, that dream remained, scarce
> fifteen minutes – a brief space, but sufficing to wring my
> whole frame with unknown anguish; to confer a nameless
> experience that had the hue, the mien, the terror, the very
> tone of a visitation from eternity. (p. 155)

The events of the novel veer uncertainly between
reality, hallucination and symbol (the holiday with the
cretin, the evening in the park), and its names lie
disturbingly somewhere between verisimilitude and
allegory (Snowe, Home, the University of Bouquin-
Moisi). Apparently new characters turn out to be
returns, as Dr John proves after some time to be
Graham Bretton, and even the school inspectors who
torment and intellectually intimidate Lucy are
recognised as the sexual harrassers of her first evening
in Labassecour. Similarly, whole episodes repeat
themselves, for the same character (as Lucy is twice
immersed in and ousted from the Bretton household)
or for different characters (Lucy writes a passionate
and cool letter to Dr John and so, with the interposition
of a third, does Paulina).

The novel's very interconnectedness seems to bring

it close to another kind of instability, to derangement; its narrative organisation suggests a kind of paranoia, a delusion of reference in which random events and chance meetings are seen to carry personalised messages for the protagonist.[2] Lucy repeatedly encounters such mysterious signs that reinforce her sense, at once narrative truth and psychological delusion, that she is herself the centre of meaning – a sense that culminates in the hallucinatory scene of the 'secret junta' (p. 457) of enemies ranged against her in the park. I do not mean to say by this that Lucy is mad or mentally unstable, though (in feminist contexts as elsewhere) she has more than once been classified in just such terms, as 'neurotic', 'schizophrenic', 'morbid', 'obsessional';[3] indeed, it has to be conceded that she once describes herself as a 'grovelling . . . monomaniac' (p. 242). My point is rather that *Villette*, in the concentration of its interconnectedness and the intensity of its narration, brings out unusually clearly a thread of paranoia implicit in the very idea of a first-person narration and its relation to its implied reader. After all, the paranoiac is, as Naomi Schor has remarked, 'the interpretant's psychotic double'.[4] And so, here, everything over-signifies, as is clear from the example of the nun, with her many possible roles in the text and its subtexts: this figure can be interpreted as, among other things, a male lover, rival for Ginevra; a dead fiancée, rival for Paul; a figure for imperfectly repressed sexual desires; an emblem of the celibate life; the spectre of Romanticism; Lucy's alter ego and her warning; a narrative joke at the expense of its narrator; a Gothic parody; a focus of textual indeterminacy and ambiguity dissolved by means of a letter; the embodiment of Catholicism; and a spectral Lacanian Other.[5] What emerges from this plethora of interpretations is the inadequacy of interpretation itself; as Christina Crosby has put it, 'the nun "is" nothing. . . . The nun is an excess, a remainder left over in the division of meaning.'[6] Excess is, indeed, always threatening here, with storm and flood, to overwhelm the line of nineteenth-century realist narrative, with its appropriate drives toward sequence, causality and typicality. Linguistic and emotional excess break through in the invocations and imperatives, the subjunctives and interrogatives of a realist notation under stress, in the novel's bilingualism, in the narrative stases of rhapsody and figuration. Notably, too, the virulent and disproportionately prominent anti-Catholicism comes into play here, and it cannot, I think, be wholly explained by the religious context of the 1850s[7] or satisfactorily recuperated into a rationalistic feminist account of the novel, as an attack upon patriarchal institutions.[8] Those very practices which Lucy holds specific to and characteristic of Catholicism, and which most provoke her anger and distaste – that is, surveillance, confession and duplicity – are replicated and examined in the tactics she employs as spectatorial, confessional and unreliable narrator. *Villette* is a challenging and self-conscious novel that in ways such as these – as in its knowing deployment of female stereotypes, and in the obtrusive nature of its doublings and dualisms – forces upon its reader the strangeness of narration itself, and raises questions about its own methods and possibilities of signification and representation.

'As to what I said, it was no confidence, no narrative'
(p. 180)

Whether I shall turn out to be the hero of my own life, or

whether that station will be held by anybody else, these pages must show.[9]

So begins *David Copperfield*, and so (with perhaps a change of gender, from 'hero' to 'heroine') could also begin *Villette*. For if the novel commences with the narrating voice of Lucy Snowe, its opening chapters seem rather to tell the stories of Mrs Bretton, Polly Home, Miss Marchmont. It begins, as Newton has pointed out,[10] with the usual end-point of nineteenth-century heroines, with marriage *à la mode de* Dickens, child-bride and lisp and all. Brontë only makes the pain and perversity of this model of adult relationship all the clearer by having her 'child-bride' be a child of seven, and by allowing her such strong and painful feelings: it is as if Dora were to have tragic potential. Polly – whose surname, of course, is 'Home' – puts the kettle on; she is a miniaturised version of the domestic and self-abnegating woman, whose labours, like the lawn handkerchief Polly hems for her father, are besprinkled with her own blood, who caresses the 'heedless foot' (p. 27) that kicks her. Graham, in return, promises what the novel fulfils (allowing for demarcation from the servants): 'that, when he had a house of his own, she should be his housekeeper, and perhaps . . . his cook' (p. 18). Mrs Bretton, cheerful widow and indulgent mother, also serves in more bantering fashion the needs and wishes of her son. These are woman who wait: they wait passively for the father or the son to come from the outside world of masculine activity to be the centre of the home, and they wait upon him when he gets there. Also waiting is Miss Marchmont, for her lover and then for death. A Miss Havisham without the grotesquerie, she is paralysed and crippled by the loss of Frank, and her only 'best friend' is 'memory' (p. 34).

Villette, then, begins with a close look at these ladies in waiting: a daughter, a 'wife', a mother, a regretful spinster, all here displayed for the reader as the dreary scenes of 'La vie d'une femme' – Jeune Fille, Mariée, Jeune Mère, Veuve – will later be for Lucy. These, then, are the women of whom stories can be told, whose lives fall – or are made to fall – squarely within the representational conventions of the mid-nineteenth century. The interpolated stories in the novel are all recognisable fictions: Miss Marchmont's tale of love and loss, that of 'one "Charlotte" a younger sister, who . . . seemed to be on the brink of perpetrating a romantic and imprudent match' (p. 46), or of Augusta, whose marriage for money is better than working (p. 50). Lucy, however, will be among those who do not fit, who embody a question best put by Gillian Beer: 'Can the female self be expressed through plot or must it be conceived in resistance to plot?'[11] Lucy, that 'heroine of the passive verb'[12], tells us often that action and event are always forced upon her, rather than initiated by her:

> [W]ith my usual base habit of cowardice I shrank into my sloth like a snail into a shell, and alleged incapacity and impracticability as a pretext to escape action. (p. 71)

She achieves 'plot', it seems, only through the plotting of others, through the secret assignations of Ginevra Fanshawe and Alfred de Hamal, the manoeuvrings of the 'secret junta', down to M. Paul's collusion with M. Miret to make her mistress of her own school. Even those instances which might in another narrative (say, Jane Eyre's) be providential signs turn out here to have been rather elements of somebody else's plot: the door that 'seems almost spontaneously to unclose . . . as if some dissolving force had gone before me' (p. 448) has merely been left on the latch, a part of the elopement plans of Ginevra and de Hamal. Those plots are what force Lucy to relinquish the 'palsy of custom' for the 'passionate pain of change' (p. 234).

Indeed, they bring her, to a certain extent, to the same point as those waiting women of the novel's opening: to Emanuel, her redeemer; to a miniaturised marriage of her own with the 'little' M. Paul and a brief domestic interlude in the Faubourg Clotilde, 'where the houses were small' (p. 480); and to 'the three happiest years of my life' (p. 488), those years spent, precisely, waiting for the second coming of Emanuel. But this recuperation of Lucy into sequential narrative is only partial, and her particular 'female self' resists by escaping into figuration and symbol. The final storm and shipwreck of *Villette* are not unambiguously an event: they form part of a series of metaphorical ships and storms that have accompanied Lucy Snowe, and that constitute as much a commentary upon the novel's narrative possibilities as a notation of incident. Rosemary Clark-Beattie has commented of *Villette* that 'the language of what really happened never achieves the ontological priority over figurative language that we expect of realism',[13] and this is nowhere more significant than at the ending. It is often noted that this is a double ending in that it proffers and withholds both a death and a marriage in allowing for the possibilities of M. Paul's death at sea or return; but it is more radically doubled in that it does not privilege event over metaphor, sequence over figure.

Early in the novel, water in gentle movement has been established as an image of temporal sequence:

Time always flowed smoothly for me at my godmother's side; not with tumultuous swiftness, but blandly, like the gliding of a full river through a plain. (p. 2)

And this bland flow of narrative sequence is associated with the stories of women:

I will permit the reader to picture me, for the next eight years, as a bark slumbering through halcyon weather, in a harbour still as glass . . . . A great many women and girls are supposed to pass their lives something in this fashion; why not I with the rest? (p. 30)

Just such a life, indeed, is Mrs Bretton's, 'a stately ship cruising safe on smooth seas' (p. 176). Lucy, however, finds herself ejected from the slumbrous bark, forced out into the tumult:

However, it cannot be concealed that, in that case, I must somehow have fallen overboard, or that there must have been wreck at last. . . . In fine, the ship was lost, the crew perished. (p. 30)

But forced out by what? It appears that even Lucy can only conjecture event: 'I *must* . . . *have* fallen, . . . there *must have* been wreck.' Shipwreck, here, is a figure that supplants, not supplements, narrative, and that marks the troubling of the bland, smooth progress of plot.

Shipwreck is associated throughout the novel with storm, and this image in turn can crucially substitute for event, as at the crisis point in Lucy's confession. The parallel between religious and narrative confession is clearly implicit, and it is all the more striking, then, that Lucy withholds the confession itself. We do not know what she confesses, other than that it is neither 'sin' nor 'crime' (p. 158), neither 'confidence' nor 'narrative' (p. 180). This obscure confession delivers her over to storm and swoon, and it is in a state of unconsciousness that Lucy begins her plot over again. When she awakes, in the reconstructed English bedroom of the Brettons, she remarks that 'all my eye rested on struck it as spectral' (p. 161). The constant references to ghosts in the novel serve in part to animate this 'ghost plot' of the novel's attempt to convey Lucy's 'female self' in the interstices of and resistances to rational, daylight plot. That 'self' is not identical with the Lucy Snowe who pleads 'guiltless of that curse, an overheated and discursive imagination' (p. 8), as is made clear when the storm briefly rages within the narrator:

> I never had felt so strange and contradictory an inward tumult as I felt for an hour that evening. . . . However, that turmoil subsided: next day I was again Lucy Snowe. (p. 114)

It is by storm and tumult that Lucy finds herself on occasion 'obliged to live' (p. 104), to confront the 'wild and weltering deep' (p. 55) that lies outside the smooth waters of plot.

When shipwreck and storm recur, then, in the final pages of the book, they fall undecidably between the status of incident (the particularities of time and place, November and the Atlantic) and that of figure (the 'destroying angel of tempest' (p. 491), the Banshee). M. Paul's trip to the West Indies has failed to bring back a convention of marital closure such as Jamaica affords Jane Eyre. Even he cannot envisage it: ' "and when I come back" – there he left a blank' (p. 483). Lucy's closing imperatives – 'leave sunny imaginations hope. Let it be theirs to conceive . . .' (p. 491) – recall her earlier indirect address to the reader: 'I will permit the reader to picture me . . . as a bark' (p. 30). In both cases, what is allowed to readers, what they expect and can contrive, is as significant as any narration in the indicative. The ending of Lucy's narrative is most radical in its refusal to narrate. But the ending of her narration returns us to the stories to which others are entitled or condemned:

> Madame Beck prospered all the days of her life; so did Père Silas; Madame Walravens fulfilled her ninetieth year before she died. (p. 491)

Lucy shares her immersion in figure with Vashti, in an episode which again withholds event – it is never made clear *what* Vashti performs other than her own suffering – and is again returned to the sequence of narrative by catastrophe, in this case fire. Vashti, who provokes the narrator to a description 'so fervently rhapsodic as to be almost incoherent',[14] is a kind of demonic double for Lucy, and also mediates between her and a Biblical prototype. Her name is taken from the biblical Vashti, who is deposed as queen to Ahasuerus for refusing his command to display herself as a spectacle of beauty for his assembled male guests. This, I think, is the point of invoking for comparison the 'slug' (p. 255) Cleopatra. Whereas Cleopatra is an image of sensuality passively displayed (the differing responses to her of men and women being clearly noted in Lucy's comically flat, prosaic commentary), Vashti's is an active, performative passion that draws from the novel's *homme moyen sensuel*, Dr John, his 'branding judgment' (p. 256).

But Vashti and Cleopatra are only two among a series of evocations of 'woman-as-spectacle' that feature in the novel. There are also Lucy and Ginevra on stage, Lucy writing ' "for a show and to order" ' (p. 354) for the examiners on her isolated pedestal, Paulina's 'fairy-dance' (p. 277). In each of these instances, there is an interplay between women as

performers and woman as spectacle in a culture orga-
nised around the needs and desires of men. These
female performers are all too likely to encounter only
the 'branding judgment' or the look of desire. Perhaps
the male or ungendered pseudonyms of so many
nineteenth-century women writers, including Brontë's
own 'Currer Bell', are glanced at in the way Lucy's
imperfect transvestite disguise releases her briefly, on
stage, into the freedom to act 'with relish' (p. 137) a
role that allows of no judgment upon her as a woman.
Certainly Brontë occasionally longed for the prospect
of a response from readers and critics that did not pass
by way of her sex:

> I wish you did not think me a woman. I wish all reviewers
> believed 'Currer Bell' to be a man; they would be more just
> to him. You will, I know, keep measuring me by some
> standard of what you deem becoming to my sex . . . .
> Come what will, I cannot, when I write, think always of
> myself and of what is elegant and charming in femini-
> nity.[15]

Brontë's Vashti, in any case, stands in an ambivalent
relation to her Biblical prototype: she is specifically *not*
beautiful, but her apparently solo act for her audience
nonetheless constitutes a performance of passion so
inflammatory (for it is with her own fire that Dr John
brands her) that it appears to set the theatre alight. In a
sardonic commentary on the social effects of this
woman's passion, Brontë allows to her self-immolation
no more than a brief flare in the draperies. But from
their (her) ashes, as it were, there appears Paulina, the
docile and feminine child-woman who will provide the
novel's happy marital ending. Paulina's name, of
course, associates her with M. Paul, and perhaps links
his role as awaited 'redeemer' with Paulina's 'saving'

role in the progress of the narrative. Justine-Marie, the rival who comes, in the latter stages of the novel, to constitute a new focus of plot and plotting, is, after all, named 'Sauveur' (p. 355).

These catastrophes of fire and storm serve to return the novel to narrative form. In this novel, the primary spatial images are of enclosure and restriction to the point of claustrophobia: rooms, houses, *l'allée défendue*, desks, sealed caskets. Most horrific among them is the recurring image of live burial:

> Was this feeling dead? I do not know, but it was buried. Sometimes I thought the tomb unquiet, and dreamed strangely of disturbed earth, and of hair, still golden and living, obtruded through coffin chinks. (p. 358)

M. Paul is able to establish for himself a relation of storm and containment that gives priority to neither: he is, for Lucy, a 'bottled storm' (p. 150). For Lucy herself, however, containment can be a strategy for preservation as well as a confinement; it is not always done *to* her, but sometimes *by* her. Images of multiple enclosure suggest the precariousness for her of the relation of storm and form. Lucy's buried letters – even those 'mere friendly letters' (p.291) from Dr John around which fantasies of her own and of others may cluster – are wrapped in oiled silk, bound with twine, enclosed in a hermetically sealed bottle, buried, cemented over and concealed with ivy. Acting on an impulse 'similar to the impulse . . . which had induced me to visit the confessional' (p. 292), Lucy buries the letters as much to prevent them from being read, and so preserve them, as to repress feeling. Her first letter from him had already been quadruply enwrapped – in silver paper, in a case, in a box, in a drawer – before ever being read. Letters, in this novel, are strangely potent, always dangerous, and yet always vulnerable to interception and misinterpretation. Reading and writing are potentially disruptive activities that come themselves to be subject to concealment and surveillance. Boissec and Rochemorte mount a 'show-trial' (p. 395) to prove that Lucy is not the author of her own work; M. Paul plants books in Greek and Latin in her desk to test his suspicion that she is secretly possessed of languages to which she will not admit.

M. Paul censors what can be read, cutting out with his penknife the pages of the novels he lends her; Dr John censors what can be written, for Lucy and for Paulina, who both pare down the emotional content of their letters to what Paulina calls ' "a morsel of ice flavoured with ever so slight a zest of fruit or sugar" ' because his ' "tastes are so fastidious" ' (p. 372). *La vie d'une femme* or Cleopatra, a ' "being inoffensive as a shadow" ' (p. 313) or scarlet woman in ' "flaunting, giddy colours" ' (p. 329): between them, Dr John and M. Paul force Lucy into a smaller and smaller space between inhibition and exhibition, invisibility and spectacle.

Lucy's attempt to be 'the heroine of her own life', then, is narrowly circumscribed by internal and external censorship, by what the patriarchal culture in which she lives will allow to be represented of women's lives without incurring the 'branding judgment' that falls upon Vashti. Her confession goes straight to the ear of a member of the 'secret junta'; the reader whom she addresses stands to some degree as her antagonist, posited as sermonisingly religious, moralistic, sternly sagacious, frowningly stoical, sneeringly cynical or frivolously epicurean, but never, above all, as 'circumstanced like me' (p. 153). Her plight is spatially imaged when, on her way 'to assist at a lesson of "style and literature" ' (p. 234), she sees on the one side two women examining her letter for evidence of unseemly conduct, and hears on the other 'the rapid step of the Professor of Literature measuring the corridor' (p. 234); caught between the intercepted letter and the Professor of Literature, is it any wonder that Lucy sits down meekly at her desk, calls the girls to order, and prepares for instruction in 'style and literature'?

'Meess Lucy'

Whatever 'Lucy Snowe' is, it seems, it is not what you think. Although the novel appears to turn upon the narrator's repeated assertion of a unified identity ('I, Lucy Snowe'), she is as often 'nobody', 'somebody', 'anybody', 'a rising character' (p. 305), even perhaps 'a personage in disguise' (p. 304). Almost the only main character who retains her name throughout – although even she acquires some nicknames from Ginevra – she is, surely oddly, addressed even at the end, even by her lover, as ' " 'Lucy' " ' (p. 490), in inverted commas, as if it were a pseudonym. Some critics have made of this sort of elusiveness and indefinition a central theme of Brontë's work: 'woman's agonized search for social and sexual identity in a male-dominated society'.[16] Certainly it is only by a good deal of critical editing that Lucy can be turned into the kind of strong heroine that some, such as Kate Millett in her pioneering feminist study of the novel, have professed to find in her.[17] She seems rather, despite her undoubtedly forceful presence as a narrator, what Chase calls 'a character without definition, a name without identity, and a voice without origins'.[18]

Phrenology and physiognomy do not have here, for characters or for the reader, the explanatory power they have elsewhere in Brontë; M. Paul, called upon to ' "read that countenance" ' (p. 61) for Mme Beck, offers only a series of equivocations and a piece of advice that depends not at all upon judgment of her inner qualities:

> 'Engage her. If good predominates in that nature, the action will bring its own reward; if evil – eh bien! Ma cousine, ce sera toujours une bonne oeuvre.' (p. 62)

The novel's emphasis upon the interpretation of ' "signs and tokens" ' (p. 2) throws sharply into relief this unreadability of its heroine. Her role as 'a cypher' (p. 324) leaves the reader to deal, undecidably, with the secret meaning of the code and the absence of meaning of the zero.[19]

As narrator, Lucy tends towards self-characterisation by negatives: she does not have an overheated imagination, she 'could not tell how it was' that she is neither 'wretched nor terrified' on first leaving England (p. 45), she is 'no bright lady's shadow' (p. 295). On more than one occasion, she recounts with a kind of gleeful satisfaction the varying views others hold of her:

> Madame Beck esteemed me learned and blue; Miss Fanshawe, caustic, ironic, and cynical; Mr Home, a model teacher, the essence of the sedate and discreet: somewhat conventional, perhaps, too strict, limited, and scrupulous, but still the pink and pattern of governess-correctness; whilst another person, Professor Paul Emanuel to wit, never lost an opportunity of intimating his opinion that mine was rather a fiery and rash nature – adventurous,

indocile and audacious. I smiled at them all. If any one knew me, it was little Paulina Mary. (p. 298)

Though Lucy smiles at them all, defining herself once more by implicit negation, it is striking how much each of these estimates corresponds to what we see of her with each of the characters she lists. It is as if she becomes what each of them believes her to be. For Dr John, she is cool, contained, dependable:

'Lucy will sit still, I know,' said he. . . . Yes, thus adjured I think I would have sat still under a rocking crag. (p. 257)

M. Paul, on the other hand, thinks her passionate and savage, and she flares out at him on a public occasion 'in just wrath' (p. 315) or bursts into patriotic rhapsody; he calls her flirtatious, and she teases him by a silent withholding of his birthday gift, or demurely offers him a needle and noosed thread to carry out his exasperated threat of hanging her.

But in her summary of the views held by others, Lucy endorses the views of 'little Paulina Mary'; so what has little Paulina Mary to say of her? Other than mistaking her for a 'rich lady' with 'rich friends' (p. 282), this appears to be her chief comment:

'Well, I never knew what you were, nor ever thought of asking: for me, you were always Lucy Snowe.'
'And what am I now?' I could not forbear inquiring.
'Yourself, of course.' (p. 281)

So, although Lucy has a 'self', this cannot be character-ised except by her name; on occasion, even her sex does not seem to be immutable.[20] Our narrator-heroine functions more as a series, a dispersal, than as a fixed centre.

One reason why this should be so emerges in the

striking contempt often expressed towards other women, 'dolls' and 'butterflies' as they are so often described, with their apparently neat fit into their containing narratives. It has become virtually a commonplace to point out that the other women of *Villette* serve as doubles and alter egos, projections and fragments of Lucy herself.[21] Polly the child-bride and Paulina the perfect young lady, Miss Marchmont the nostalgic spinster and Mme Beck the scheming widow, Ginevra the heartless flirt and Justine-Marie the tragic lover who died young: in all these instances and others, Lucy gives a notably ambivalent account of such figures who seem to embody a series of possibilities or warnings for herself. It is momentarily chilling when this general suspicion, or even animosity, is for once acknowledged:

> I liked her. It is not a declaration I have often made concerning my acquaintance in the course of this book: the reader will bear with it for once. (p. 367)

But what these characters also represent are the known and knowable narratives of woman, the stories that seem of necessity to generate certain kinds of characters. If Lucy, in exile from such stories, is to have doubles, then the truest ones, it seems to me, are Vashti and the nun. Vashti: 'something neither of woman nor of man'; 'scarcely a substance herself', she 'grapples to conflict with abstractions' (p. 254). The nun: a woman (Justine-Marie) and/or a man (Alfred de Hamal), a spectre and/or a substance, she is finally ungraspable beneath the veil:

> I shook her loose – the mystery! And down she fell – down all round me – down in shreds and fragments – and I trode upon her. (p. 467)

Whether this be inscrutability or vacancy, it suggests something that Lucy shares: a 'female self', to recall Beer's phrase, that is not encompassed or displayed by narrative.

On occasion, nevertheless, Lucy appeals to the idea of natural character in her process of self-definition by negation. Dr John, for example, 'wanted always to give me a role not mine. Nature and I opposed him' (p. 314). The role in question is that of 'officious soubrette in a love drama' (p. 314), so that it is miscasting to which Lucy objects. The use of theatrical metaphor here is important, and picks up the strain of theatricality (acting and disguise) that runs through the novel. Lucy rejects the flat, insipid images of women proposed by static art – Cleopatra and *La vie d'une femme* – and seems to propose, in their stead, the dangerous but appealing freedom of the actress.[22] She discovers in herself 'a keen relish for dramatic expression' (p. 137) that she immediately rejects in favour of the role of audience, spectator, 'a mere looker-on at life' (p. 137). But if the performance of Vashti, and the risk of the 'branding judgment', are not for Lucy, she nevertheless acts out her allotted roles in other people's stories: learned and blue, caustic and cynical, sedate and discreet, fiery and rash. And like Vashti, she 'grapples to conflict with abstractions' (p. 254), staging her own interior drama of female personifications (Liberty, Hope, Adversity, even the 'evil, grovelling and repellent' Real (p. 105)) in struggle and suffering.

Near the beginning of the novel, before her departure for Labassecour, Lucy is 'overcome by a terrible oppression' and a sense of her position visits her 'like a ghost' (p. 41). She poses a series of questions:

What was I doing here alone in great London? What

should I do on the morrow? What prospects had I in life?
What friends had I on earth? Whence did I come? Whither
should I go? What should I do? (p. 41)

These are at once the fundamental questions of
narrative impulsion and the fundamental questions of
originating identity. As her life falls outside the conventional stories of women, so too her 'female self' falls
outside such definitions of identity. ' "Unheroined",
unsweetened', as Heilman puts it,[23] she is one of those
whom Brontë claimed as her own heroines: 'Mel-
chisedecs – without father, without mother, without
descent, having neither beginning nor days nor end of
life'.[24]

This relative downgrading of identity is, of course,
enabled by the fact that Lucy Snowe is an orphaned,
displaced, exiled narrator. Her narration takes her to a
country she despises, among a 'swinish multitude'
(p. 78) of Catholics, 'robust in body, feeble in soul, fat,
ruddy, hale, joyous, ignorant, unthinking, unquestion-
ing' (p. 122), in thrall to 'monkish extravagances'
(p. 111) and 'priest-craft' (p. 112). She is throughout
convinced of the superiority of the English lady and of
Protestantism, and, provoked by the symmetrical pre-
judices of M. Paul, she cries out ' "Vive l'Angleterre,
l'Histoire et les Héros! A bas la France, la Fiction et les
Faquins!" ' (p. 337), spontaneously alliterating in the
heat of the moment. And yet: she stays in Labassecour,
she acquires respect for Mme Beck, the Catholic
M. Paul becomes her 'Christian hero' (p. 394) despite
his 'points of resemblance to Napoleon Bonaparte'
(p. 344), and her authorship enlists her in the service of
Fiction at least as much as of Histoire. It is of England
that she speaks as a 'wilderness', both in its 'flat, rich
middle' (p. 39) and in the 'Babylon and . . . Wilderness'

of London (p. 40). It seems to belong to Dr John, 'his
own England' (p. 256). It is England – very specifically
identified, in a novel full of figurative females, as the
*Father*land (p. 56) – that excludes her, and this rejection
is symbolically repeated on foreign soil in a marriage
that unites Home and Bretton (here, surely, to be read
as 'Britain') to the exclusion of Lucy Snowe. The double
plots of exile and xenophobia are a means by which
Lucy constitutes herself, primarily, as difference *from*:
an English lady in a foreign country, an English speaker
in a second language, a Protestant in a Catholic
society.[25]

Lucy's orphanhood and exile are, of course, in one
sense the basis of her dispossession and privation,
though the curiously *given* quality of her isolation and
misery suggests that they reflect it as much as cause it.
But this very privation is also a kind of freedom, for it
seems to place Lucy irretrievably outside the determining structures of class, family and patrilineage. She has
and will discover no family, other than the surrogate
Brettons; she has and will discover no inheritance
other than a small bequest from a female employer,
delayed and diverted by the latter's male kin. And Lucy
and Paul's foreignness for one another also serves to
render them effectively classless for one another.
Nevertheless, this 'freedom' has clear limits; it exists,
that is to say, only within the space created for it,
under the name of the 'surplus woman', by the
structures of patriarchal power. As one of those 'surplus woman' whose fate had begun to pose a problem,
in the mid-nineteenth century, to expectations of a
serene passage from father to husband, she is from the
first treated on the basis of her sex above all else, with
none of the gallantry that Ginevra and Paulina attract

by virtue of their beauty: cheated by the water-
man, pursued by the sexual harrassers, employed by
Mme Beck who gets 'thrice the work out of me she
had extracted from Mr Wilson, at half the expense'
(p. 76).

The literal families of *Villette* are fragmented and
dismembered, with fathers dead (Lucy's, Graham's, the
Beck children's, Justine-Marie's) or absent (Polly's,
Ginevra's). Such families are the focus of an inturned
sexual feeling that also embodies the power of the male
within the family; in Dr John's jocular vows to turn his
mother out of her chair and replace her with a wife, or
in M. de Bassompierre's handshake that seems to
' "crush Graham's hand to the bone" ' (p. 431), there is
as much of flirtation and jealousy, and as much exercise
of power, as in anything that occurs between the
novel's lovers. But if the literal families contain their
threats within their own charmed circles, Lucy must
confront family configurations of affinity and power
that continue to reject or thwart her: Father England
and the Mother Church, or Père Silas and 'Mère
Walravens' (p. 392).

Unlike Jane Eyre, though, Lucy's movement is not
from family home to family home, but from job to job.
Nina Auerbach makes an interesting case for *Villette* as
an example of a patriarchal social order hijacked by the
Amazons, stressing its female rulers and its insistence
upon communities of women at the expense of
families.[26] For her, Lucy Snowe is initiated into the
necessity and practices of power as part of a succession
that has already passed from Mme Walravens to Mme
Beck. But the novel's powerful women are all nonetheless dutiful daughters, surviving and exercising their
power in and through an alliance with a status quo that

requires the constant sexual and intellectual policing of other women. The truest 'Amazon' in *Villette* would appear to be that Mme Panache whose story testifies briefly to the Napoleonic qualities, good and bad, of M. Paul. Free-striding, confident, voluble, Mme Panache finds herself unceremoniously ousted from the community of women when she fails to please its most benevolent patriarch, M. Paul. Lucy's modest criticism – that the 'laurels of this victory' do not become him (p. 345) – is not altogether cancelled by his later efforts on her behalf. But this victory is not only over Mme Panache; it is also over the community of women. Relations within the school, in any case, are less communitarian than combative; Lucy finds herself more than once engaged in a 'challenge of strength' (p. 72) with Mme Beck, and she initially takes up this challenge by a more literal version of the same kind of struggle, locking her most disruptive pupil in the classroom cupboard to prove herself to her new employer. The school is no protected enclave of sisterliness: relations between women are shown to pass through the power or the desire of men, as Lucy's stage wooing of Ginevra depends upon her 'longing to eclipse the "Ours", *i.e.*, Dr John' (p. 136). As Auerbach stresses, the school is itself a political arena, but it is also indissolubly linked with state (the 'secret junta' holds its final meeting at the national fete of Labassecour), with church (Lucy's pupils take a distance from her when she is suspected of proselytising Protestant tendencies) and, of course, with patriarchal power. The relationship of Lucy and M. Paul appears, briefly, to put them, in their new school, out of reach of their society, as they come to accept differences between them that are not hierarchies, as they displace the relations of master and pupil to accommodate those of friends or brother and sister, as they evade patrimony by the interchange of gifts. But their idyll in the Faubourg Clotilde under 'such moonlight as fell on Eden' (p. 487) has no future. The symbolic family (Père Silas and Mère Walravens), marital exchange, patrilineal inheritance, reassert themselves in M. Paul's errand: 'Let him bring them an Indian fortune: they would give him in return a young bride and a rich inheritance' (p. 463). The idyll of Paul and Lucy has its brief moment only because he opts, not for the *Antigua*, but for the *Paul et Virginie*[27] of fantasied romantic transcendence. Nevertheless, it is the trip to Guadeloupe that introduces into *Villette* a shadowy narrative of patrilineage and imperialism, a narrative that will carry the lovers' future beyond the reach of 'sunny imaginations' into the 'wild south-west storm' (p. 491) that marks the end, for Lucy Snowe, of the telling of stories.

Notes

Introduction: Plotting the ground

1. Editions of the novels of Charlotte Brontë cited are as follows: *The Professor*, Everyman's Library (London: Dent, 1985); *Jane Eyre*, ed. Margaret Smith, World's Classics (Oxford: Oxford University Press, 1980; rpt 1987); *Shirley*, eds Herbert Rosengarten and Margaret Smith, World's Classics (Oxford: Oxford University Press, 1981); *Villette*, Everyman's Library (London: Dent, 1983).
2. F.R. Leavis, *The Great Tradition* (1948; Harmondsworth: Penguin, 1972), p. 39.
3. Anon., review of *Shirley*, *Athenaeum*, 3 November 1849, 1107–9, partially reprinted in Miriam Allott, ed., *The Brontës: The Critical Heritage*, The Critical Heritage Series (London: Routledge & Kegan Paul, 1974) pp. 122–4 (p. 124).
4. Anon., review of *Villette*, *Guardian*, 23 February 1853, 128–9, partially reprinted in Allott, *The Critical Heritage*, pp. 193–4 (p. 194).
5. Ruth Gounelas, 'Charlotte Brontë and the critics: attitudes to the female qualities in her writing', *Journal of the*

123

Australasian Universities Language and Literature Association, 62 (1984), 151.

6. See, for example, Anon., review of *Jane Eyre*, *Era*, 14 November 1847, 9, partially reprinted in Allott, *The Critical Heritage*, pp. 78–80 (p. 79).

7. Anon., review of *Jane Eyre*, *Christian Remembrancer*, April 1848, 396–409, partially reprinted in Allott, *The Critical Heritage*, pp. 88–92 (p. 89).

8. See, respectively, Anon., review of *Shirley*, *Atlas*, 3 November 1849, 696–7, partially reprinted in Allott, *The Critical Heritage*, pp. 119–21; (pp. 120–1); [Alban Fonblanque], review of *Shirley*, *Examiner*, 3 November 1849, 692–4, partially reprinted in Allott, *The Critical Heritage*, pp. 125–9 (p. 126); [William Howitt], review of *Shirley*, *Standard of Freedom*, 10 November 1849, 2, partially reprinted in Allott, *The Critical Heritage*, pp. 133–5 (p. 133).

9. Anon., review of *Jane Eyre*, *Christian Remembrancer*, in Allott, *The Critical Heritage*, p. 89.

10. [G.H.Lewes], review of *Jane Eyre*, *Fraser's Magazine*, December 1847, 686–95, partially reprinted in Allott, *The Critical Heritage*, pp. 83–7 (pp. 85, 86).

11. Pauline Nestor, *Charlotte Brontë*, Women Writers (London: Macmillan Educational, 1987), p. 39 remarks that 'the masculine perception of Crimsworth in *The Professor* is too often implausible, particularly in its detailed acquaintance with feminine minutiae.'

12. [Elizabeth Rigby], review of *Jane Eyre*, *Quarterly Review*, December 1848, 153–85, partially reprinted in Allott, *The Critical Heritage*, pp. 105–12 (p. 111).

13. [Elizabeth Rigby], review of *Jane Eyre*, *Quarterly Review*, in Allott, *The Critical Heritage*, p. 111.

14. [James Lorimer], review of *Jane Eyre*, *North British Review*, August 1849, 455–93, partially reprinted in Allott, *The Critical Heritage*, pp. 113–6 (p. 116).

15. Review of *Jane Eyre*, *Fraser's Magazine*, in Allott, *The Critical Heritage*, p. 84.

16. [G.H.Lewes], review of *Shirley*, *Edinburgh Review*, 91

(1850), 153–73, partially reprinted in Allott, *The Critical Heritage*, pp. 160–70 (p. 163).

17. 'To G.H. Lewes', [January 1850], in *The Brontës: Their Lives, Friendships and Correspondence*, eds T.J. Wise and J.A. Symington, 4 vols. (1933; Oxford: Basil Blackwell 1980), III, p. 67.

18. Leslie Stephen, *Hours in a Library*, 4 vols. (1892; revised edn, London: Smith, Elder, 1907), III, pp. 272–312.

19. Virginia Woolf, '*Jane Eyre* and *Wuthering Heights*', (1925), in *Virginia Woolf: Women and Writing*, ed. Michèle Barrett (London: The Women's Press, 1979), p. 129.

20. Virginia Woolf, 'Women and fiction', (1929), in *Virginia Woolf: Women and Writing*, ed. Barrett, p. 47. I quote this passage, not in order to participate in the feminist attacks on Woolf that have sometimes taken place, but rather to illustrate how, even in a sympathetic and often pioneeringly feminist critic like Woolf, reading Brontë exclusively as a woman writing has tended in the past to produce concentration on the 'faults' of her writing. It is worth pointing out too that in the omitted portion of the last sentence quoted, Woolf also includes race and class among those elements in which 'disability' is liable to produce 'weakness', 'distortion' and special pleading.

21. Anon., review of *Shirley*, *Athenaeum*, 3 November 1849, 1107–9, partially reprinted in Allott, *The Critical Heritage*, pp. 122–4 (p. 123).

22. Matthew Arnold, 'To Mrs Forster', 14 April 1853, in *Letters of Matthew Arnold, 1848–1888*, ed. G.W.E. Russell, 4 vols. (London: Macmillan, 1895), I, p. 29.

23. Gounelas, 'Charlotte Brontë and the critics', p. 157.

24. Elizabeth Gaskell, *The Life of Charlotte Brontë* (1857; London: Dent, 1974) has the particular interest of being probably the first biography of one woman novelist by another. Winifred Gérin, *Charlotte Brontë: The Evolution of Genius* (Oxford: Oxford University Press, 1976) is probably the standard work. Tom Winnifrith, *The Brontës and their Background* (London: Macmillan 1973) and Margot

Peters, *Unquiet Soul: A Biography of Charlotte Brontë* (London: Hodder & Stoughton, 1975) are both of interest, while Hélène Moglen, *Charlotte Brontë: The Self Conceived* (New York: W.W. Norton, 1976) takes a more feminist line. John Maynard, *Charlotte Brontë and Sexuality* (Cambridge: Cambridge University Press, 1984) contains an appendix arguing against the view that Brontë was pregnant at the time of her death.

25. Fanny E. Ratchford, *The Brontës' Web of Childhood* (1941; New York: Russell & Russell, 1964) remains a useful account of the early writings. Christine Alexander has made the field her own through her editions of the juvenilia, and her *The Early Writings of Charlotte Brontë* (Oxford: Basil Blackwell, 1983) is now the standard work. Many of the critical works on Brontë include chapters on the juvenilia, but the suggestive brief discussion in Karen Chase, *Eros and Psyche: The Representation of Personality in Charlotte Brontë, Charles Dickens, George Eliot* (New York: Methuen, 1984), pp. 7–24, and the chapter in Maynard, *Brontë and Sexuality*, pp. 40–71, are particularly good. John Kucich, 'Passionate reserve and reserved passion in the works of Charlotte Brontë', *ELH*, 52 (1985), 913–37, also makes some interesting remarks on the early writings.

26. See Toril Moi, *Sexual/Textual Politics: Feminist Literary Theory*, New Accents (London: Methuen, 1985), pp. 19–88.

27. Elizabeth Deeds Ermarth, *Realism and Consensus in the English Novel* (Princeton, NJ: Princeton University Press, 1983), p. 65.

28. Rachel Blau DuPlessis, *Writing Beyond the Ending: Narrative Strategies of Twentieth-century Women Writers*, Everywoman Studies in History, Literature, and Culture (Bloomington, Indiana: Indiana University Press, 1985), p. 3.

29. Patricia Yaeger, *Honey-mad Women: Emancipatory Strategies in Women's Writing*, Gender and Culture (New York: Columbia University Press, 1988), pp. 37, 38 and 35 respectively.

30. E. Ann Kaplan, *Women and Film: Both Sides of the Camera* (London: Methuen, 1983), p. 31. The preliminary definition of the gaze occurs on p. 15. See also Laura Mulvey, 'Visual pleasure and narrative cinema', *Screen*, 16, 3 (1975), 6–18. An influential formulation of this argument in relation to painting can be found in John Berger, *Ways of Seeing* (Harmondsworth: BBC/Penguin Books, 1972; rpt 1985), pp. 45–64. The issue of the look in *Jane Eyre* is discussed in Peter J. Bellis, 'In the window-seat: vision and power in *Jane Eyre*', *ELH*, 54 (1987), 639–52.

31. I do not forget here that the stories of heroines in themselves demand the obscuring of other stories; see the discussions of *Jane Eyre* and of *Shirley* in Chapters 3 and 4 below.

32. Nancy K. Miller, *Subject to Change: Reading Feminist Writing*, Gender and Culture (New York: Columbia University Press, 1988), pp. 158–9, n. 9.

33. Nancy K. Miller, *Subject to Change*, pp. 8–9. I see the force of Bryan S. Turner's argument, in *The Body and Society: Explorations in Social Theory* (Oxford: Basil Blackwell, 1984), in favour of replacing 'patriarchal' by 'patrist' in such contexts, but 'patriarchal' is the preferred term in so much of contemporary feminist writing that I have decided to retain it here.

34. Eugène Forçade, '*Jane Eyre*: autobiographie', *Revue des deux mondes*, 31 October 1848, 471–94, as reprinted in Allott, *The Critical Heritage*, pp. 100–104 (p. 103).

35. Review of *Shirley*, *Edinburgh Review*, in Allott, *The Critical Heritage*, p. 164.

36. Anon, review of *Villette*, *Athenaeum*, 12 February 1853, 186–8; partially reprinted in Allott, *The Critical Heritage*, pp. 187–90 (p. 190).

37. Peter Brooks, *Reading for the Plot: Design and Intention in Narrative* (Oxford: Clarendon Press, 1984), pp. 6–7.

38. Tim Dolin, ' "A long familiar inscription": *The Lifted Veil* and the perception of plot in George Eliot', unpublished dissertation, University of Western Australia, 1987, p. 6. Some of my argument here draws upon Dolin's.

39. Ermarth, *Realism and Consensus*, p. 64.
40. Ermarth, *Realism and Consensus*, p. 65.
41. Fredric Jameson, *The Political Unconscious: Narrative as a Socially Symbolic Act* (1981; London: Methuen, 1983), p. 102.
42. Leslie W. Rabine, *Reading the Romantic Heroine: Text, History, Ideology* (Ann Arbor: University of Michigan Press, 1985), p. 5.
43. Brooks, *Reading for the Plot*, p. 350, n. 3.
44. Dolin, ' "A long familiar inscription" ', p. 7.
45. DuPlessis, *Writing Beyond the Ending*, p. 3.
46. Brooks, *Reading for the Plot*, p. 5.
47. Nancy K. Miller, *Subject to Change*, p. 208.
48. Jameson, *The Political Unconscious*, p. 86.
49. Cf. DuPlessis, pp. 4–7.
50. Nancy Armstrong, *Desire and Domestic Fiction: A Political History of the Novel* (New York: Oxford University Press, 1987), p. 11. See also, for a related objection, the Introduction to John Kucich, *Repression in Victorian Fiction: Charlotte Brontë, George Eliot, and Charles Dickens* (London: University of California Press, 1987), pp. 1–33.
51. D.A. Miller, *Narrative and its Discontents: Problems of Closure in the Traditional Novel* (Princeton, NJ: Princeton University Press, 1981), p. 264.
52. Carol Ohmann, 'Historical reality and "Divine Appointment" in Charlotte Brontë's fiction', *Signs: Journal of Women in Culture and Society*, 2, 4 (Summer, 1977), 757–78.
53. Robert B. Heilman, 'Charlotte Brontë's "New" Gothic', in *From Jane Austen to Joseph Conrad: Essays Collected in Memory of James T. Hillhouse*, eds Robert C. Rathburn and Martin Steinmann, Jr (Minneapolis: University of Minnesota Press, 1958), pp. 118–32 (p. 131).
54. DuPlessis, *Writing Beyond the Ending*, p. 44.
55. First argued in Richard Chase, 'The Brontës, or, myth domesticated', in *Forms of Modern Fiction: Essays Collected in Honor of Joseph Warren Beach*, ed. William Van O'Connor (Minneapolis: University of Minnesota Press, 1948), pp. 102–19.

56. Charles Burkhart, *Charlotte Brontë: A Psychosexual Study of her Novels* (London: Gollancz, 1973), p. 75.
57. Carolyn Heilbrun, *Towards a Recognition of Androgyny* (New York: Harper Colophon, 1974), p. 59.
58. Ohmann, 'Historical reality and "Divine Appointment" ', 763.
59. W.A. Craik, *The Brontë Novels* (London: Methuen, 1968), p. 123.
60. D.A. Miller, *Narrative and its Discontents*, pp. 269–70.
61. Judith Lowder Newton, *Women, Power, and Subversion: Social Strategies in British Fiction, 1778–1860* (Athens, Ga.: University of Georgia Press, 1981), p. 124. Kate Millett similarly suggests that romance and success meet only in fantasy: *Sexual Politics* (London: Abacus, 1972), p. 141.
62. Leo Bersani, *A Future for Astyanax: Character and Desire in Literature* (London: Marion Boyars, 1978), p. x.

Chapter One: The Professor

1. Charlotte Brontë, *The Professor*, Everyman's Library (London: Dent, 1985), p. 186. Further references to the novel are to this edition and will be given in the text.
2. For a discussion of the Victorian Orientalisation of sex and sexualisation of 'the Orient', see Joanna de Groot, ' "Sex" and "Race": the construction of language and image in the nineteenth century', in *Sexuality and Subordination: Interdisciplinary Studies of Gender in the Nineteenth Century*, eds. Susan Mendus and Jane Rendall (London: Routledge, 1989), pp. 89–128.
3. For a discussion of this issue, see Kathleen Blake, *Love and the Woman Question in Victorian Literature: The Art of Self-Postponement* (Brighton: Harvester Press, 1983), pp. 101–45.
4. Contrast, for example, *Jane Eyre*, World's Classics (Oxford: Oxford University Press, 1975), pp. 306–7.

5. Cf. John Maynard, *Charlotte Brontë and Sexuality* (Cambridge: Cambridge University Press, 1984), pp. 80–5.
6. For example, in Sandra M. Gilbert and Susan Gubar, *The Madwoman in the Attic: The Woman Writer and the Nineteenth-Century Literary Imagination* (New Haven: Yale University Press, 1979), p. 319.
7. Pauline Nestor, *Charlotte Brontë*, Women Writers (London: Macmillan Education, 1987), p. 47.
8. Cf. Maynard, *Brontë and Sexuality*, pp. 87–9, and Robert Keefe, *Charlotte Brontë's World of Death* (Austin: University of Texas Press, 1979), pp. 87–9.
9. Gilbert and Gubar, *Madwoman in the Attic*, p. 333.
10. Dianne F. Sadoff, *Monsters of Affection: Dickens, Eliot, and Brontë on Fatherhood* (Baltimore: Johns Hopkins University Press, 1982), p. 149.
11. The other versions of the Oedipal story involve, first, William's relationship with his brother and his mother's portrait, and secondly, his involvement with Pelet and Zoraïde. See Maynard, *Brontë and Sexuality*, pp. 77–8, and Keefe, *Brontë's World of Death*, p. 83.
12. Franco Moretti, *The Way of the World: The 'Bildungsroman' in European Culture* (London: Verso, 1987), p. 15.
13. Terry Eagleton, *Myths of Power: A Marxist Study of the Brontës* (London: Macmillan, 1975), p. 33.
14. I use the term 'rape/seduction' here to designate a coincidence possible in fantasy. Of course it is vital to keep these categories distinct in fact.
15. Hélène Moglen, *Charlotte Brontë: The Self Conceived* (New York: W.W. Norton, 1976), p. 104. Cf. Nestor, *Charlotte Brontë*, pp. 41–2.
16. Gilbert and Gubar, *Madwoman in the Attic*, p. 318.
17. Eagleton, *Myths of Power*, p. 42.
18. John Kucich, 'Passionate reserve and reserved passion in the works of Charlotte Brontë', *ELH* 52 (1985), 913–37.
19. Cf. Annette Tromly, *The Cover of the Mask: The Autobiographers in Charlotte Brontë's Fiction*, English Literary Studies no. 26 (Victoria, BC: University of Victoria, 1982), p. 29.

20. See, for example, Eagleton, *Myths of Power*, p. 41; Keefe, *Brontë's World of Death*, p. 85.
21. Cf. Moglen, *The Self Conceived*, p. 98.
22. Gilbert and Gubar, *Madwoman in the Attic*, p. 331.
23. 'But it is not with a view to distinction that you should cultivate this talent, if you consult your own happiness. . . . The day dreams in which you habitually indulge are likely to induce a distempered state of mind; and, in proportion as all the ordinary uses of the world seem to you flat and unprofitable, you will be unfitted for them without becoming fitted for anything else. Literature cannot be the business of a woman's life, and it ought not to be. The more she is engaged in her proper duties, the less leisure she will have for it, even as an accomplishment and recreation. To those duties you have not yet been called, and when you are you will be less eager for celebrity. You will not seek in imagination for excitement . . .': Robert Southey, 'To Charlotte Brontë', March 1837, in *The Brontës: Their Lives, Friendships and Correspondence*, eds T.J. Wise and J.A. Symington, 4 vols (1933; Oxford: Basil Blackwell, 1980), I, p. 155.
24. Gilbert and Gubar, *Madwoman in the Attic*, p. 327.
25. Gilbert and Gubar, *Madwoman in the Attic*, p. 326.

Chapter Two: Jane Eyre

1. Charlotte Brontë, *Jane Eyre*, ed. Margaret Smith, World's Classics (Oxford: Oxford University Press, 1980: reprinted 1987), p. 33. All page references are to this edition and will hereafter be given in the text.
2. Joseph Prescott, '*Jane Eyre*: a romantic exemplum with a difference', in *Twelve Original Essays on Great English Novels*, ed. Charles Shapiro (Detroit: Wayne State University Press, 1960), p. 91.

3. Terry Eagleton, *Myths of Power: A Marxist Study of the Brontës* (London: Macmillan, 1975), p. 18.
4. Hermione Lee, 'Emblems and enigmas in *Jane Eyre*', *English*, 30 (Autumn, 1981), 223.
5. Gayatri Chakravorty Spivak, 'Three women's texts and a critique of imperialism', *Critical Inquiry*, 12 (1985), 243–61, 245; reprinted in *'Race', Writing, and Difference*, ed. Henry Louis Gates, Jr (Chicago: University of Chicago Press, 1986), pp. 262–80. For a critique of Spivak's argument, see Laura E. Donaldson, 'The Miranda complex: colonialism and the question of feminist reading', *Diacritics*, 18 (1988), 65–77.
6. Respectively, Lee R. Edwards, *Psyche as Hero: Female Heroism and Fictional Form* (Middletown, Conn.: Wesleyan University Press, 1984), p. 76; Jina Politi, '*Jane Eyre* classified', *Literature and History*, 8 (1982), 56; Judith Weissman, *Half Savage and Hardy and Free: Women and Rural Radicalism in the Nineteenth-century Novel* (Middletown, Conn.: Wesleyan University Press, 1987), p. 84.
7. See, respectively, Peter J. Bellis, 'In the window-seat: vision and power in *Jane Eyre*', *ELH*, 54 (1987), 639–52; Politi, '*Jane Eyre* class-ified'; Spivak, 'Three women's texts'. Jean Rhys, *Wide Sargasso Sea* (London: Andre Deutsch, 1966), is of course a kind of 'restoration' of Bertha's story.
8. I am using the phrase, of course, to invoke the issues raised in the important feminist discussion of the novel in Sandra M. Gilbert and Susan Gubar, *The Madwoman in the Attic: The Woman Writer and the Nineteenth-century Literary Imagination* (New Haven: Yale University Press, 1979).
9. Cf. Philip W. Martin, *Mad Women in Romantic Writing* (Brighton: Harvester Press, 1987), pp. 124–39. James Cowles Pritchard's theory of 'moral madness', on which Brontë based the pathology of Bertha Rochester, is discussed in Peter Grudin, 'Jane and the other Mrs Rochester: excess and restraint in *Jane Eyre*', *Novel*, 10 (1977), 145–57.

10. The only other 'Quakerish' character in the novel is Grace Poole (p. 157), and this forms part of an interesting series of connections between the two characters.

11. Among the most useful of the genre-based accounts of the novel are the following: a stimulating, if unsympathetic and gender-blind, account of *Jane Eyre* as *Bildungsroman* in Franco Moretti, *The Way of the World: the 'Bildungsroman' in European Culture* (London: Verso, 1987); on Gothic elements, Robert B. Heilman, 'Charlotte Brontë's "New" Gothic', in *From Jane Austen to Joseph Conrad: Essays Collected in Memory of James T. Hillhouse*, eds Robert C. Rathburn and Martin Steinmann, Jr (Minneapolis: University of Minnesota Press, 1958), pp. 118–32, reprinted in *The Brontës: A Collection of Critical Essays*, ed. Ian Gregor, Twentieth Century Views (Englewood Cliffs, NJ: Prentice Hall Inc., 1970), pp. 96–109, and Marxist-Feminist Literature Collective, 'Women's writing: "Jane Eyre", "Shirley", "Villette", "Aurora Leigh",' in *1848: the Sociology of Literature. Proceedings of the Essex Conference on the Sociology of Literature, July 1977*, eds Francis Barker *et al.* (Colchester: University of Essex, 1978), pp. 185–206; on folk- and fairy-tale, Paula Sullivan, 'Fairy tale elements in *Jane Eyre*', *Journal of Popular Culture*, 12 (1978), 61–74; on the governess novel, Harriet Björk, *The Language of Truth: Charlotte Brontë, the Woman Question, and the Novel*, Lund Studies in English 47 (Lund: Gleerup, 1974) and Inga-Stina Ewbank, *Their Proper Sphere: A Study of the Brontë Sisters as Early-Victorian Female Novelists* (London: Edward Arnold, 1966); on allegory and emblem-books, Lee, 'Emblems and Enigmas'.

12. Most famously, in Adrienne Rich, '*Jane Eyre*: the temptations of a motherless woman', *MS 2* (Oct., 1973); reprinted in her *On Lies, Secrets, and Silence: Selected Prose 1966–1978* (New York: W.W. Norton, 1979), pp. 89–106.

13. Elaine Showalter, *A Literature of their Own: British Women Novelists from Brontë to Lessing* (Princeton, NJ: Princeton University Press, 1977), pp. 112–24.

14. I am thinking here of such matters as Jane's appropriation of the words of Christ on p. 20 and of Biblical quotation, e.g. on p. 453.
15. *The Madwoman in the Attic*, p. 364. We might see in Jane's flight from Thornfield to the heath a version of that 'female plot' outlined by Sandra M. Gilbert, 'Life's empty pack: notes toward a literary Daughteronomy', *Critical Inquiry*, 11 (1985), 355–84: the woman who 'flees from culture (her father's palace) to nature (the great wood), trying to transform herself into a creature of nature . . . rather than acquiesce in the extreme demands culture is making upon her' (377). Gilbert suggests, however, that this flight is commonly motivated by the need 'to escape paternal desire'.
16. Cf. Sullivan, 'Fairy tale elements', 68.
17. Helena Michie, *The Flesh Made Word: Female Figures and Women's Bodies* (New York: Oxford University Press, 1987), pp. 12–29, traces the depiction of women's hunger and its relation to sexuality in Victorian writing. Her claim that, like other nineteenth-century heroines, Jane is 'never actually seen eating' (p. 15) is surely inaccurate, however.
18. Cf. Margaret Homans, *Bearing the Word: Language and Female Experience in Nineteenth-century Women's Writing*, Women in Culture and Society (Chicago: Chicago University Press, 1986), pp. 84–99.
19. Politi, '*Jane Eyre* class-ified', 64.
20. Although Edwards thinks Jane a 'spiritual aristocrat' (*Psyche as Hero*, p. 76), Politi and Eagleton are surely right to see her as, respectively, occupying the 'space . . . of the unaccommodated *petit-bourgeois*' ('*Jane Eyre* class-ified', 57) and as representative of a meritocratic bourgeois myth (*Myths of Power*, p. 26). I think it should be noted, however, that her marriage to Rochester constitutes a move into the rural gentry.
21. The narrative implications of phrenology and physiognomy are very well discussed in Karen Chase,

Eros and Psyche: The Representation of Personality in Charlotte Brontë, Charles Dickens, and George Eliot (New York: Methuen, 1984), pp. 47–65.

22. Politi, '*Jane Eyre* class-ified', 65.

23. Among these, the following are particularly worth attention: Gilbert and Gubar, *The Madwoman in the Attic*, pp. 336–71; Pauline Nestor, *Charlotte Brontë*, Women Writers (London: Macmillan Education, 1987), pp. 50–67; Rich, 'Motherless woman'; Ruth Bernard Yeazell, 'More true than real: Jane Eyre's "Mysterious Summons" ', *NCF*, 29 (1974), 127–43.

24. Jerome Beaty, '*Jane Eyre* and genre,' *Genre*, 10 (1977), 654.

25. Cf. Chase, *Eros and Psyche*, p. 11.

26. Doreen Roberts, '*Jane Eyre* and the warped system of things', in *Reading the Victorian Novel: Detail into Form*, ed. Ian Gregor (London: Vision, 1980), p. 138.

27. Chase, *Eros and Psyche*, pp. 66–91.

28. Nancy Pell, 'Resistance, rebellion, and marriage: the economics of *Jane Eyre*', *NCF*, 31 (1977), 397–420.

29. For a further consideration of these issues, see my 'George Eliot and the end of realism,' in *Women Reading Women's Writing*, ed. Sue Roe (Brighton: Harvester Press, 1987), pp. 13–35.

Chapter Three: Shirley

1. Charlotte Brontë, 'To W.S. Williams', 26 July 1849, in *The Brontës: Their Lives, Friendships and Correspondence*, eds T.J. Wise and J.A. Symington, 4 vols (1933; Oxford: Basil Blackwell, 1980), III, p. 9; cf. Charlotte Brontë, *Shirley*, eds Herbert Rosengarten and Margaret Smith, World's Classics (Oxford: Oxford University Press, 1981), p. 399. Further references to the novel are to this edition and will be given in the text.

2. Mary Taylor, 'To Charlotte Brontë', 25 April 1850, Wise and Symington, III, p. 104.

3. See also p. 241.
4. Cf. Sandra M. Gilbert and Susan Gubar, *The Madwoman in the Attic: The Woman Writer and the Nineteenth-century Literary Imagination* (New Haven: Yale University Press, 1979), pp. 372–98.
5. Pauline Nestor, *Female Friendships and Communities: Charlotte Brontë, George Eliot, Elizabeth Gaskell* (Oxford: Clarendon Press, 1985), pp. 112–24.
6. Tess Cosslett, *Woman to Woman: Female Friendship in Victorian Fiction* (Brighton: Harvester Press, 1988), p. 11.
7. Patricia Parker, *Literary Fat Ladies: Rhetoric, Gender, Property* (New York: Methuen, 1987), *passim*. Parker does not discuss *Shirley*.
8. Margaret Kirkham has discussed *Shirley* in relation to Rousseau in 'Reading "The Brontës" ', *Women Reading Women's Writing*, ed. Sue Roe (Brighton: Harvester Press, 1987), pp. 66–75.
9. Gilbert and Gubar, *Madwoman in the Attic*, p. 382.
10. Cf. Joseph Kestner, *Protest and Reform: The British Social Narrative by Women, 1827–1867* (London: Methuen, 1985), p. 132.
11. Cf. Nestor, *Female Friendships*, p. 124. Nestor seems, however, to have changed her mind on this point, since she later writes of the novel's 'swaggering satiric manner', ' "masculine" by default': Pauline Nestor, *Charlotte Brontë*, Women Writers (London: Macmillan Education, 1987), p. 69.
12. William Thackeray, *Vanity Fair*, ed. J.I.M. Stewart (1968; Harmondsworth: Penguin 1983), p. 738.
13. Leslie W. Rabine, *Reading the Romantic Heroine: Text, History, Ideology* (Ann Arbor: University of Michigan Press, 1985), p. 112.
14. I have discussed this point in relation to some women writers of the 1890s in *Thomas Hardy and Women: Sexual Ideology and Narrative Form* (Brighton: Harvester Press, 1982), pp. 63–97.
15. See also pp. 101, 153, 164, 435.

16. Nestor, *Female Friendships*, p. 104. Nestor takes this phrase from Elizabeth Barrett Browning, *Aurora Leigh*, I, 40.

17. Rosemarie Bodenheimer, *The Politics of Story in Victorian Social Fiction* (Ithaca: Cornell University Press, 1988), p. 19. For a discussion of women's writing in the sub-genre of the industrial novel, see Kestner, *Protest and Reform*.

18. *Coriolanus*, I, i.

19. Terry Eagleton, *Myths of Power: A Marxist Study of the Brontës* (London: Macmillan, 1975), pp. 45–60, argues convincingly that 'Chartism is the unspoken subject of *Shirley*' (p. 45). His discussion of class issues in *Shirley* is surely definitive. Nevertheless, since, for the Eagleton of this book, gender and sexual relations are finally always metaphorical, always a displacement (and, as such, to some extent at least a guilty evasion) of the determining reality of class relations, there remains, I think, something for feminists to say even in this area.

20. Cf. Hélène Moglen, *Charlotte Brontë: The Self Conceived* (New York: W.W. Norton, 1976), p. 163.

21. Eagleton, *Myths of Power*, pp. 47, 49.

22. Helen Taylor, 'Class and gender in Charlotte Brontë's *Shirley*,' *Feminist Review*, no. 1 (1979), 83–93.

Chapter Four: Villette

1. Charlotte Brontë, *Villette*, Everyman's Library (London: Dent, 1983), p. 60. Further references to the novel are to this edition and will be given in the text.

2. ' "Delusion of reference" ' is the term Freud uses for 'the interpretation of immaterial accidental indications given by other people', in *The Psychopathology of Everyday Life*, trans. Alan Tyson, Volume 5 of the Pelican Freud Library (Harmondsworth: Penguin, 1976), p. 316.

3. See, for example, Hélène Moglen, *Charlotte Brontë: The*

Self Conceived (New York: W.W. Norton, 1976), p. 196 ('neurotic rationalization'); Sandra M. Gilbert and Susan Gubar, *The Madwoman in the Attic: The Woman Writer and the Nineteenth-century Literary Imagination* (New Haven: Yale University Press, 1979), p. 416 ('Lucy's schizophrenia'); Janice Carlisle, 'The face in the mirror: *Villette* and the conventions of autobiography', *ELH*, 46 (1979), 277 ('The morbid narrator'); Kate Millett, *Sexual Politics* (London: Abacus, 1971), p. 140 ('a compulsive mirror obsession'). The other diagnosis not infrequently made of Lucy is that of frigidity; see, for instance, Russell M. Goldfarb, *Sexual Repression in Victorian Literature* (Lewisburg: Bucknell University Press, 1970), pp. 139–57.

4. Naomi Schor, *Reading in Detail: Aesthetics and the Feminine* (London: Methuen, 1987), p. 125. Here and elsewhere, Schor calls for a psychoanalytic feminist hermenuetics founded upon female paranoia; see also her *Breaking the Chain: Women, Theory, and French Realist Fiction*, Gender and Culture Series (New York: Columbia University Press, 1985), pp. 149–62. By contrast, Donald D. Stone, *The Romantic Impulse in Victorian Fiction* (Cambridge, Mass.: Harvard University Press, 1980), pp. 126–7, cites paranoia only as part of the psychology of the character Lucy Snowe.

5. Particularly useful discussions of the nun's role in the novel are to be found in: Christina Crosby, 'Charlotte Brontë's haunted text', *SEL* 24 (1984), 701–15; Mary Jacobus, 'The buried letter: feminism and romanticism in *Villette*', in *Women Writing and Writing About Women*, ed. Mary Jacobus (London: Croom Helm, 1979), pp. 42–60; and Dianne F. Sadoff, *Monsters of Affection: Dickens, Eliot, and Brontë on Fatherhood* (Baltimore: Johns Hopkins University Press, 1982), pp. 143–58.

6. Crosby, 'Haunted text', 709.

7. An excellent critical discussion of *Villette* in this context is Rosemary Clark-Beattie, 'Fables of rebellion: anti-catholicism and the structure of *Villette*', *ELH*, 53 (1986), 821–47.

8. For example, M.A. Blom, 'Charlotte Brontë: feminist manquée', *Bucknell Review*, 21 (1973), 87–102.

9. Charles Dickens, *The Personal History of David Copperfield*, ed. Trevor Blount (1966; Harmondsworth: Penguin, 1983), p. 49.

10. Judith Lowder Newton, *Women, Power, and Subversion: Social Strategies in British Fiction, 1778–1860* (Athens, Ga.: University of Georgia Press, 1981), p. 86.

11. Gillian Beer, 'Beyond determinism: George Eliot and Virginia Woolf,' in *Women Writing and Writing About Women*, ed. Jacobus, p. 80. The appositeness of this quotation was drawn to my attention by Tim Dolin, 'Unsafe passage: the journey to Villette', unpublished paper, 1987.

12. Annette Tromly, *The Cover of the Mask: The Autobiographers in Charlotte Brontë's Fiction*, English Literary Studies no. 26 (Victoria, BC: University of Victoria, 1982), p. 68.

13. Clark-Beattie, 'Fables of rebellion,' 829.

14. Gilbert and Gubar, *Madwoman in the Attic*, p. 422.

15. 'To G.H. Lewes', 1 November 1849; *The Brontës: Their Lives, Friendships and Correspondence*, eds T.J. Wise and J.A. Symington, 4 vols (1933; Oxford: Basil Blackwell, 1980), III, p. 31.

16. Blom, 'Feminist manquée', 87.

17. For example, Millett, *Sexual Politics*, pp. 139–47.

18. Karen Chase, *Eros and Psyche: The Representation of Personality in Charlotte Brontë, Charles Dickens, George Eliot* (New York: Methuen, 1984), p. 67.

19. This ambiguity is examined very effectively in Karen Lawrence, 'The cypher: disclosure and reticence in *Villette*', NCL, 42 (1988), 448–66.

20. Cf. Crosby, 'Haunted text,' 701–15.

21. Good discussions of this include Chase, *Eros and Psyche*, pp. 66–70, and Gilbert and Gubar, *Madwoman in the Attic*, pp. 399–440.

22. Cf. Rachel M. Brownstein, *Becoming a Heroine: Reading About Women in Novels* (1982; Harmondsworth: Penguin,

1984), pp. 154–81. On acting in *Villette*, see Joseph Litvak, 'Charlotte Brontë and the scene of instruction: authority and subversion in *Villette*', *NCL*, 42 (1988), 467–89.

23. Robert B. Heilman, 'Charlotte Brontë's "New" Gothic', in *From Jane Austen to Joseph Conrad: Essays Collected in Memory of James T. Hillhouse*, eds Robert C. Rathburn and Martin Steinmann, Jr (Minneapolis: University of Minnesota Press, 1958), p. 119.

24. 'To Hartley Coleridge', quoted in John Kucich, 'Passionate reserve and reserved passion in the works of Charlotte Brontë', *ELH*, 52 (1985), 924.

25. Cf. Clark-Beattie, 'Fables of rebellion'.

26. Nina Auerbach, *Communities of Women: An Idea in Fiction* (Cambridge, Mass.: Harvard University Press, 1978), pp. 97–113.

27. Jacques-Henri-Bernardin de Saint-Pierre's *Paul et Virginie* (1788) sets its similar plot elements in a more exoticised and romanticised context.

Bibliography of works cited

Alexander, Christine, *The Early Writings of Charlotte Brontë* (Oxford: Basil Blackwell, 1983).

Allott, Miriam (ed.), *The Brontës: The Critical Heritage*, The Critical Heritage Series (London: Routledge & Kegan Paul, 1974).

Armstrong, Nancy, *Desire and Domestic Fiction: A Political History of the Novel* (New York: Oxford University Press, 1987).

Arnold, Matthew, *Letters of Matthew Arnold, 1848–1888*, ed. G.W.E. Russell, 4 vols (London: Macmillan, 1895).

Auerbach, Nina, *Communities of Women: An Idea in Fiction* (Cambridge, Mass.: Harvard University Press, 1978).

Beaty, Jerome, '*Jane Eyre* and genre', *Genre*, 10 (1977), 619–54.

Beer, Gillian, 'Beyond determinism: George Eliot and Virginia Woolf', in *Women Writing and Writing About Women*, ed. Mary Jacobus (London: Croom Helm, 1979), pp. 80–99.

Bellis, Peter J., 'In the window-seat: vision and power in *Jane Eyre*', *ELH*, 54 (1987), 639–52.

Berger, John, *Ways of Seeing* (Harmondsworth: BBC/Penguin Books, 1972); rpt 1985.

Bersani, Leo, *A Future for Astyanax: Character and Desire in Literature* (London: Marion Boyars, 1978).

Björk, Harriet, *The Language of Truth: Charlotte Brontë, the Woman Question, and the Novel*, Lund Studies in English 47

(Lund: Gleerup, 1974).

Blake, Kathleen, *Love and the Woman Question in Victorian Literature: The Art of Self-postponement* (Brighton: Harvester Press, 1983).

Blom, M.A. 'Charlotte Brontë: feminist manquée', *Bucknell Review*, 21 (1973), 87–102.

Bodenheimer, Rosemarie, *The Politics of Story in Victorian Social Fiction* (Ithaca: Cornell University Press, 1988).

Boumelha, Penny, 'George Eliot and the end of realism', in *Women Reading Women's Writing*, ed. Sue Roe (Brighton: Harvester Press, 1987), pp. 13–35.

Boumelha, Penny, *Thomas Hardy and Women: Sexual Ideology and Narrative Form* (Brighton: Harvester Press, 1982); rpt 1984.

Brontë, Charlotte, *The Professor*, Everyman's Library (London: Dent, 1985).

Brontë, Charlotte, *Jane Eyre*, ed. Margaret Smith, World's Classics (Oxford: Oxford University Press, 1980); rpt 1987.

Brontë, Charlotte, *Shirley*, eds. Herbert Rosengarten and Margaret Smith, World's Classics (Oxford: Oxford University Press, 1981).

Brontë, Charlotte, *Villette*, Everyman's Library (London: Dent, 1983).

Brooks, Peter, *Reading for the Plot: Design and Intention in Narrative* (Oxford: Clarendon Press, 1984).

Brownstein, Rachel M., *Becoming a Heroine: Reading About Women in Novels* (1982; Harmondsworth: Penguin, 1984).

Burkhart, Charles, *Charlotte Brontë: A Psychosexual Study of her Novels* (London: Gollancz, 1973).

Carlisle, Janice, 'The face in the mirror: *Villette* and the conventions of autobiography', *ELH*, 46 (1979), 262–89.

Chase, Karen, *Eros and Psyche: The Representation of Personality in Charlotte Brontë, Charles Dickens, George Eliot* (New York: Methuen, 1984).

Chase, Richard, 'The Brontës, or, myth domesticated', in *Forms of Modern Fiction: Essays Collected in Honor of Joseph Warren Beach*, ed. William Van O'Connor (Minneapolis: University of Minnesota Press, 1948), pp. 102–19.

Bibliography of works cited

Clark-Beattie, Rosemary, 'Fables of rebellion: anti-Catholicism and the structure of *Villette*', *ELH*, 53 (1986), 821–47.

Cosslett, Tess, *Woman to Woman: Female Friendship in Victorian Fiction* (Brighton: Harvester Press, 1988).

Craik, W.A., *The Brontë Novels* (London: Methuen, 1968).

Crosby, Christina, 'Charlotte Brontë's haunted text', *SEL*, 24 (1984), 701–15.

de Groot, Joanna, ' "Sex" and "Race": the construction of language and image in the nineteenth century', in *Sexuality and Subordination: Interdisciplinary Studies of Gender in the Nineteenth Century*, eds. Susan Mendus and Jane Randall, (London: Routledge, 1989), pp. 89–128.

Dickens, Charles, *The Personal History of David Copperfield*, ed. Trevor Blount (1966; Harmondsworth: Penguin, 1983).

Dolin, Tim, ' "A long familiar inscription": *The Lifted Veil* and the perception of plot in George Eliot', unpublished dissertation, University of Western Australia, 1987.

Dolin, Tim, 'Unsafe passage: the journey to *Villette*', unpublished paper, 1987.

Donaldson, Laura E., 'The Miranda complex: colonialism and the question of feminist reading', *Diacritics*, 18 (1988), 65–77.

DuPlessis, Rachel Blau, *Writing Beyond the Ending: Narrative Strategies of Twentieth-century Women writers*, Everywoman Studies in History, Literature, and Culture (Bloomington: Indiana University Press, 1985).

Eagleton, Terry, *Myths of Power: A Marxist Study of the Brontës* (London: Macmillan, 1975).

Edwards, Lee R., *Psyche as Hero: Female Heroism and Fictional Form* (Middletown, Conn.: Wesleyan University Press, 1984).

Ermarth, Elizabeth Deeds, *Realism and Consensus in the English Novel* (Princeton, NJ: Princeton University Press, 1983).

Ewbank, Inga-Stina, *Their Proper Sphere: A Study of the Brontë Sisters as Early-Victorian Female Novelists* (London: Edward Arnold, 1966).

Freud, Sigmund, *The Psychopathology of Everyday Life*, trans. Alan

Tyson, vol. 5 of the Pelican Freud Library (Harmondsworth: Penguin, 1976).

Gaskell, Elizabeth, *The Life of Charlotte Brontë* (Oxford: Oxford University Press, 1974).

Gérin, Winifred, *Charlotte Brontë: The Evolution of Genius*, (Oxford: Oxford University Press, 1976).

Gilbert, Sandra M., 'Life's empty pack: notes toward a literary Daughteronomy', *Critical Inquiry*, 11 (1985), 355–84.

Gilbert, Sandra M. and Susan Gubar, *The Madwoman in the Attic: The Woman Writer and the Nineteenth-century Literary Imagination* (New Haven: Yale University Press, 1979).

Goldfarb, Russell M., *Sexual Repression in Victorian Literature* (Lewisburg, Penn.: Bucknell University Press, 1970).

Gounelas, Ruth, 'Charlotte Brontë and the critics: attitudes to the female qualities in her writing', *Journal of the Australasian Universities Language and Literature Association*, 62 (1984), 151–70.

Gregor, Ian (ed.), *The Brontës: A Collection of Critical Essays*, Twentieth Century Views (Englewood Cliffs, NJ: Prentice Hall, Inc., 1970).

Grudin, Peter, 'Jane and the other Mrs Rochester: excess and restraint in *Jane Eyre*', *Novel*, 10 (1977), 145–57.

Heilbrun, Carolyn, *Towards a Recognition of Androgyny* (New York: Harper Colophon, 1974).

Heilman, Robert B., 'Charlotte Brontë's "New" Gothic', in *From Jane Austen to Joseph Conrad: Essays Collected in Memory of James T. Hillhouse*, eds. Robert C. Rathburn and Martin Steinmann, Jr. (Minneapolis: University of Minnesota Press, 1958), pp. 118–32, reprinted in *The Brontës: A Collection of Critical Essays*, ed. Ian Gregor, pp. 96–109.

Homans, Margaret, *Bearing the Word: Language and Female Experience in Nineteenth-century Women's Writing*, Women in Culture and Society (Chicago: Chicago University Press, 1986).

Jacobus, Mary, 'The buried letter: feminism and romanticism in *Villette*', in *Women Writing and Writing About Women*, ed. Mary Jacobus (London: Croom Helm, 1979), pp. 42–60.

Jameson, Fredric, *The Political Unconscious: Narrative as a Socially Symbolic Act* (1981; London: Methuen, 1983).

Kaplan, E. Ann, *Women and Film: Both Sides of the Camera* (London: Methuen, 1983).

Keefe, Robert, *Charlotte Brontë's World of Death* (Austin: University of Texas Press, 1979).

Kestner, Joseph, *Protest and Reform: The British Social Narrative by Women, 1827-1867* (London: Methuen, 1985).

Kirkham, Margaret, 'Reading "The Brontës"', in *Women Reading Women's Writing*, ed. Sue Roe (Brighton: Harvester Press, 1987), pp. 66-75.

Kucich, John, 'Passionate reserve and reserved passion in the works of Charlotte Brontë', *ELH*, 52 (1985), 913-37.

Kucich, John, *Repression in Victorian Fiction: Charlotte Brontë, George Eliot, and Charles Dickens* (London: University of California Press, 1987).

Lawrence, Karen, 'The cypher: disclosure and reticence in *Villette*', *NCL*, 42 (1988), 448-66.

Leavis, F.R., *The Great Tradition* (1948; Harmondsworth: Penguin, 1972).

Lee, Hermione, 'Emblems and enigmas in *Jane Eyre*', *English*, 30 (1981), 233-55.

Litvak, Joseph, 'Charlotte Brontë and the scene of instruction: authority and subversion in *Villette*', *NCL*, 42 (1988), 467-89.

Martin, Philip W., *Mad Women in Romantic Writing* (Brighton: Harvester Press, 1987).

Marxist-Feminist Literature Collective, 'Women's writing: "Jane Eyre", "Shirley", "Villette", "Aurora Leigh"', in *1848: The Sociology of Literature. Proceedings of the Essex Conference on the Sociology of Literature, July 1977*, eds. Francis Barker *et al.* (Colchester: University of Essex, 1978), pp. 185-206.

Maynard, John, *Charlotte Brontë and Sexuality* (Cambridge: Cambridge University Press, 1984).

Michie, Helena, *The Flesh Made Word: Female Figures and Women's Bodies* (New York: Oxford University Press, 1987).

Miller, D.A., *Narrative and its Discontents: Problems of Closure in the*

Bibliography of works cited

Traditional Novel (Princeton, NJ: Princeton University Press, 1981).

Miller, Nancy K., *Subject to Change: Reading Feminist Writing*, Gender and Culture (New York: Columbia University Press, 1988).

Millett, Kate, *Sexual Politics* (London: Abacus, 1971).

Moglen, Hélène, *Charlotte Brontë: The Self Conceived* (New York: W.W. Norton, 1976).

Moi, Toril, *Sexual/Textual Politics: Feminist Literary Theory*, New Accents (London: Methuen, 1985).

Moretti, Franco, *The Way of the World: The 'Bildungsroman' in European Culture* (London: Verso, 1987).

Mulvey, Laura, 'Visual pleasure and narrative cinema', *Screen*, 16, 3 (1975), 6–18.

Nestor, Pauline, *Charlotte Brontë*, Women Writers (London: Macmillan Educational, 1987).

Nestor, Pauline, *Female Friendships and Communities: Charlotte Brontë, George Eliot, Elizabeth Gaskell* (Oxford: Clarendon Press, 1985).

Newton, Judith Lowder, *Women, Power and Subversion: Social Strategies in British Fiction, 1778–1860* (Athens: University of Georgia Press, 1981).

Ohmann, Carol, 'Historical reality and "Divine Appointment" in Charlotte Brontë's fiction', *Signs: Journal of Women in Culture and Society*, 2 (1977), 757–78.

Parker, Patricia, *Literary Fat Ladies: Rhetoric, Gender, Property* (New York: Methuen, 1987).

Pell, Nancy, 'Resistance, rebellion, and marriage: the economics of *Jane Eyre*', *NCF*, 31 (1977), 397–420.

Peters, Margot, *Unquiet Soul: A Biography of Charlotte Brontë* (London: Hodder & Stoughton, 1975).

Politi, Jina, '*Jane Eyre* class-ified', *Literature and History*, 8 (1982), 56–66.

Prescott, Joseph, '*Jane Eyre*: a romantic exemplum with a difference', in *Twelve Original Essays on Great English Novels*, ed. Charles Shapiro (Detroit: Wayne State University Press, 1960), pp. 87–102.

Rabine, Leslie W., *Reading the Romantic Heroine: Text, History, Ideology* (Ann Arbor: University of Michigan Press, 1985).

Ratchford, Fanny E., *The Brontës' Web of Childhood* (1941; New York: Russell & Russell, 1964).

Rhys, Jean, *Wide Sargasso Sea* (London: Andre Deutsch, 1966).

Rich, Adrienne, 'Jane Eyre: the temptations of a motherless woman', *MS* 2 (Oct., 1973), reprinted in her *On Lies, Secrets, and Silence: Selected Prose 1966–1978* (New York: W.W. Norton 1979), pp. 89–106.

Roberts, Doreen, 'Jane Eyre and the warped system of things', in *Reading the Victorian Novel: Detail into Form*, ed. Ian Gregor (London: Vision, 1980), pp. 131–49.

Sadoff, Dianne F., *Monsters of Affection: Dickens, Eliot, and Brontë on Fatherhood* (Baltimore: Johns Hopkins University Press, 1982).

Schor, Naomi, *Breaking the Chain: Women, Theory, and French Realist Fiction*, Gender and Culture Series (New York: Columbia University Press, 1985).

Schor, Naomi, *Reading in Detail: Aesthetics and the Feminine* (New York: Methuen, 1987).

Showalter, Elaine, *A Literature of their Own: British Women Novelists from Brontë to Lessing* (Princeton, NJ: Princeton University Press, 1977).

Spivak, Gayatri Chakravorty, 'Three women's texts and a critique of imperialism', *Critical Inquiry*, 12 (1985), 243–61, reprinted in *'Race', Writing, and Difference*, ed. Henry Louis Gates, Jr. (Chicago: University of Chicago Press, 1986), pp. 262–80.

Stephen, Leslie, *Hours in a Library*, 4 vols., 1892; rev. edn (London: Smith, Elder, 1907).

Stone, Donald D., *The Romantic Impulse in Victorian Fiction* (Cambridge, Mass.: Harvard University Press, 1980).

Sullivan, Paula, 'Fairy tale elements in Jane Eyre', *Journal of Popular Culture*, 12 (1978), 61–74.

Taylor, Helen, 'Class and gender in Charlotte Brontë's Shirley', *Feminist Review*, no. 1 (1979), 83–93.

Thackeray, William, *Vanity Fair*, ed. J.I.M. Stewart (1968; Harmondsworth: Penguin, 1983).

Tromly, Annette, *The Cover of the Mask: The Autobiographers in Charlotte Brontë's Fiction*, English Literary Studies no. 26 (Victoria, BC: University of Victoria, 1982).

Turner, Bryan S., *The Body and Society: Explorations in Social Theory* (Oxford: Basil Blackwell, 1984).

Weissman, Judith, *Half Savage and Hardy and Free: Women and Rural Radicalism in the Nineteenth-century Novel* (Middletown, Conn.: Wesleyan University Press, 1987).

Winnifrith, Tom, *The Brontës and their Background* (London: Macmillan, 1973).

Wise, T.J. and J.A. Symington (eds.), *The Brontës: Their Lives, Friendships and Correspondence*, 4 vols. (1933; Oxford: Basil Blackwell, 1980).

Woolf, Virginia, *Virginia Woolf: Women and Writing*, ed. Michèle Barrett (London: The Women's Press, 1979).

Yaeger, Patricia, *Honey-mad Women: Emancipatory Strategies in Women's Writing*, Gender and Culture (New York: Columbia University Press, 1988).

Yeazell, Ruth Bernard, 'More true than real: Jane Eyre's "Mysterious Summons" ', *NCF*, 29 (1974), 127–43.

Index

acting, 117, 139
allegory, 30, 83, 101
androgyny, 43, 47, 48, 51,
52
anti-Catholicism, 34–5, 103,
118
Armstrong, Nancy, 19
Arnold, Matthew, 6
artist, woman as, 9, 53
Auerbach, Nina, 120, 121
Austen, Jane (*Pride and
Prejudice*), 15
autobiography, 9, 63

ballad, 63
Beaty, Jerome, 74
Beer, Gillian, 105, 117
Bersani, Leo, 37
Bildungsroman, 14, 44, 46, 63,
74, 133
Bodenheimer, Rosemarie,
94

body, 39, 40, 44, 70–1, 95
Brontë, Charlotte, 4, 6–7,
57, 59, 63, 79, 110
'Currer Bell', 3, 110
correspondence, 5, 55–6,
79, 110, 131
Jane Eyre, 1, 2, 3, 6, 8, 9,
10, 11, 12, 16, 18, 19,
24–8, 37, 47, 52, 54,
58–77, 78, 79, 80,
105, 108
juvenilia, 7, 126
The Professor, 3, 9, 10, 20–
3, 36–7, 38–57
Shirley, 1, 2, 3, 4, 5, 6, 8,
9, 10, 11, 12, 13, 28–
32, 36–7, 54, 78–99
Villette, 1, 8, 9, 10, 16, 17,
32–6, 51, 54, 75, 77,
79, 100–22
Brontë, Emily, 1, 7
Wuthering Heights, 36, 47

Brooks, Peter, 13, 15, 16
Bunyan, John (*The Pilgrim's Progress*), 40, 86
Burkhart, Charles, 27

Chartism, 95
Chase, Karen, 76, 113
Cinderella, 47
Clark-Beattie, Rosemary, 106
class, 60, 61, 63, 64, 65, 69, 70, 72, 80-1, 93-9, 125, 134
communities of women, 66, 68, 91-2, 120-1
Coriolanus, 95
Cosslett, Tess, 83
Craik, Wendy, 28
Crosby, Christina, 103

desire, 12, 15, 18, 20, 21, 24, 29, 30, 32, 37, 77
Dickens, Charles, 104
David Copperfield, 104
Great Expectations, 104
Dolin, Tim, 13
DuPlessis, Rachel, Blau, 16, 25

Eagleton, Terry, 47, 51, 59, 98, 134, 137
Edwards, Lee R., 60, 73
Eliot, George, 4, 6
Middlemarch, 6
The Mill on the Floss, 15
emigration, 78, 79, 81, 97-8
Ermarth, Elizabeth, 9, 13-14
Eve, 12, 87, 88, 89, 92

fairy tales, 47, 63, 77, 133

family 64, 65, 66, 69, 119-22
'feminine' writing, 2-7
figuration, 102, 103, 106, 107, 108, 109
Forcade, Eugène, 12-13
Freud, Sigmund, 137

gaze, male, 10, 11, 127
'gender signatures', 11, 12
Gilbert, Sandra, 134
and S. M. Gubar, 49, 67, 84, 132, 137
Gothic, 8, 18, 77, 133
Gounelas, Ruth 2, 7

Heilman, Robert B., 118
historical novel, 14, 32, 85, 92-4

illness, 92, 95
industrial novel, 85, 97, 98, 137

Jamaica, 61-2, 108
Jameson, Fredric, 14-15, 18

Kaplan, E. Ann, 10-11
Kucich, John, 51

language, women and, 10, 11, 12, 56, 84, 85, 111
Leavis, F. R., 1
Lee, Hermione, 60
Lewes, G. H., 4-6, 8, 13
Luddism, 29, 32, 95

marriage, 18, 22, 23, 24, 25, 26, 27, 28, 29, 30, 35, 52, 69, 72, 92, 93, 94

masculinity, 2–5, 47, 48,
  49
master-slave relationships,
  48, 50, 51, 52
matriarchy, 64, 66, 67, 68
Miller, D. A., 19, 31
Miller, Nancy K., 11–12, 17
Millett, Kate, 113, 129, 138
Milton, John, 12, 87
Moglen, Hélène, 48, 137
Moretti, Franco, 46
motherhood, 4, 30, 67, 90,
  92

nature and the natural, 67,
  68, 71, 90, 92, 97,
  114
Nestor, Pauline, 3, 82, 92,
  124, 136
Newton, Judith Lowder,
  104
Nicholls, A. B., 57

Ohmann, Carol, 22, 28
Orientalisation of sex, 42,
  129

paranoia, 41, 102, 138
Parker, Patricia, 83
Pell, Nancy, 77
phrenology, 39, 71, 95, 113,
  134
physiognomy, 39, 71, 114,
  134
plot, 8, 12–37, 44, 69, 73, 74,
  76, 83, 96, 104, 105,
  106, 107, 108, 109,
  110, 111, 122
  'female' plot, 15, 16, 18,
    19, 20
  of *Bildung*, 19, 20, 22, 23,

  24, 26, 34, 35, 36, 44
  of desire, 15, 19, 20, 25
Politi, Jina, 69, 72, 73, 134
providence, 59, 73, 105
providential narrative, 24,
  69, 74

Rabine, Leslie, 15, 90
race, 8, 60, 61, 62, 79, 125
reading, women and, 16,
  110–11
realism, 13, 16, 69, 77, 82,
  103, 106
religion, women and, 67,
  88, 89, 90
reviews, 1–7, 12
rhapsody, 12, 29, 31, 82,
  109
Rhys, Jean, 132
romance, 8, 18, 19, 20, 21,
  22, 23, 24, 25, 26, 28,
  29, 31, 32, 33, 34, 35,
  63, 77, 97, 129

Sadoff, Dianne, 46
St Paul, 77, 87
Saint-Pierre, Jacques-Henri-
  Bernardin de (*Paul et
  Virginie*), 122, 140
Schor, Naomi, 102, 138
sex, 29, 41, 42, 43, 44, 50
Showalter, Elaine, 66
slavery, 62
Southey, Robert, 57, 131
Spivak, Gayatri
  Chakravorty, 60
spectacle, woman as, 109,
  110
Stephen, Leslie, 6, 7

Taylor, Helen, 98

Taylor, Mary, 79
Thackeray, William, 78, 86
  Vanity Fair, 86-7
Turner, Bryan S., 127

utopianism, 25, 31, 37, 82, 83

vocation, 19, 20, 21, 22, 23,
  25, 26, 31, 33, 35, 36,
  63, 74-5

Weissman, Judith, 60, 73
Woolf, Virginia, 7, 125
work, women and, 90-1, 98,
  119-20, 121
writers, women as, 4, 5, 6,
  10, 11, 15, 16, 17, 18,
  54, 55, 56, 111-12

Yaeger, Patricia, 10